The Narcissist and the Awakening

Paris Stephenson

BOOKS

Winchester, UK
Washington, USA

JOHN HUNT PUBLISHING

First published by O-Books, 2023
O-Books is an imprint of John Hunt Publishing Ltd., 3 East St., Alresford,
Hampshire SO24 9EE, UK
office@jhpbooks.com
www.johnhuntpublishing.com
www.o-books.com

For distributor details and how to order please visit the 'Ordering' section on our website.

Text copyright: Paris Stephenson 2022

ISBN: 978 1 80341 281 8
978 1 80341 282 5 (ebook)
Library of Congress Control Number: 2022939085

A CIP catalogue record for this book is available from the British Library.

Design: Lapiz Digital Services

UK: Printed and bound by CPI Group (UK) Ltd, Croydon, CR0 4YY
Printed in North America by CPI GPS partners

The author of this book does not dispense medical advice or
prescribe the use of any technique as a form of treatment for
physical, emotional, or medical problems without the advice of a
physician, either directly or indirectly. The intent of the author
is only to offer information of a general nature to help you in
your quest for emotional and spiritual well-being. In the event
you use any of the information in this book for yourself, which is
your constitutional right, the author and the publisher assume no
responsibility for your actions.

We operate a distinctive and ethical publishing philosophy in
all areas of our business, from our global network of authors to
production and worldwide distribution.

Contents

Introduction

Who this book is for

This book is for anyone who has experienced emotional abuse and wants to find out more. I hope that it will not only give you information, but also be a source of guidance, empowerment and love while you heal.

I decided to write this book because, although there is now more awareness in Western society regarding emotional abuse, there is more to this topic than is commonly expressed. I understand how sensitive a topic this is, and have tried to approach all aspects of it in a respectful and dignified manner.

So please allow me to take you on a journey to discover the psychology of how narcissistic abuse works. Most importantly, I want to explore the spiritual side of this, and the spiritual reasons why narcissists may come into your life. In sharing with you, my hope is that this insight can assist you in healing and in promoting the never-ending expression and presence of oneness within you.

Some sections will apply to everyone; however, because we all have different experiences, please take what resonates with you and leave what doesn't. You may not view yourself as religious or spiritual and that is completely fine. I only ask that you open your heart while reading and soften any predisposed ideas you have, as this book offers you an alternative approach to healing and to taking back your power.

Some background

I came into this world on 1 April 1990. Born to an Asian mother and Caribbean father, I grew up in south-east London in a fairly strict household and had a fairly average childhood, although I felt as though I never really fitted into my family, because

I couldn't quite meet up to my parents' high expectations. Growing up, I felt increasingly alone, with no one to relate to, and being an only child for the first ten years of my life.

As I grew into a young woman I began to rebel as a means of escapism, and took to hanging around with what can only be described as unsavoury characters. I did manage to further my education, going to college and studying health and social care. I then obtained a full-time job in a brain injury rehabilitation unit, where I worked as a senior rehabilitation assistant, supporting different clients for several years. I was fully committed to my role and enjoyed my work as I was able to see the difference I could make helping people. I am now a qualified Reiki practitioner, and am training to become a counsellor. My passion has always been to support others in one way or another.

I began writing to help me cope with life; this started with journaling and writing about my feelings. As I began to experience my spiritual awakening, I realised how much I enjoyed writing and that I could use this as a method of reaching out to those who have had a similar experience to myself. First, though, I went through some dark times.

My awakening began in 2020, although really it started a couple years before this. I remember sitting in my bathroom every day, asking God for help. Although I had a good life, I still wasn't happy. One day I took matters into my own hands – by this I mean that I was consciously seeking out a dark experience, something where I could be promiscuous. This was in 2019, but what I didn't realise at the time was that what I was doing was already a part of what my soul had planned. My karma in this lifetime is within close partnerships and I was about to experience my first Saturn return. My higher self said, 'You are now ready. Ready for an experience that will pull you into the deep depths of darkness.'

Gradually I learned that this was so that I could pull myself out – and when I came out I felt transformed, a changed person.

2

I remember the day I felt a higher presence shine over me – it was the most beautiful thing I have ever felt. I didn't want it to go away. From that moment, I had many questions. I began communicating with my guides, asking them for direction. I must admit I was becoming quite driven about this, even obsessed, but this is part of what I'm dealing with in this lifetime, and it gave me the energy to make great progress and to manifest my vision. And as I began to research, I got my answers through meditation, dreaming, reading, non-verbal communication like a strong feeling (intuition), listening to others, understanding my birth chart, numerology, human design, seeing synchronicities, and so on. All of these are ways that we can receive direction or insight from our higher self. The entry number on my birth certificate is 111, a significant number in numerology – known as the angel number, it indicates awakenings and a new life journey under the guidance of your angels.

As for the abuse, I was aware of it when it started, meaning that I knew it was wrong but was not so aware of how it would affect me as I had never experienced anything like it before (not in this lifetime anyway). You could say I was naïve. The experience with my narcissist was different in the sense that I chose him. I too can display some narcissistic characteristics, and I believe that to some degree we all can, especially in our younger years. We are all battling with our egos, and finding ourselves. Overall it boils down to making the right choices.

What followed were the next steps of the awakening; the dark night of the soul came next. I had to work through every stage, repeating certain stages, until I was able to let go. This process for me lasted over the course of two to three years. I became interested in spiritual arts because what I was experiencing was not something I had heard about much, and at the time I didn't really know what was happening. I had to go through the experience of having my auric field damaged to a high degree so that I could begin to repair it. To describe how it felt, for me it was as if some heavy forces were pulling down on me, and I would then experience panic attacks. I also experienced periods of feeling withdrawn from my environment. All of this may sound like symptoms of post-traumatic stress disorder or depression but for me I knew something spiritual was happening inside of me.

My experience with my narcissist was pretty condensed, as my encounter with him lasted for a period of just two years. Although it was fairly brief, I was still able to take much from it – in fact, it was only the start of an incredible journey of self-awareness. When I realised what was happening, it took a lot of bravery on my part to deal with it. I had to look at the parts of myself I had been running away from for years, and to accept that many of the decisions I had made in the past were not always serving my best interest.

Gradually I learned that this is the path of self-love and has nothing to do with conventional spirituality as laid down by others. It's to do with looking at yourself in a way you may never have done before. Prior to my experience with a narcissist, I had little direction on where I wanted my life to go. I was heavily addicted to cannabis, and feeding my addiction took up all of my free time. As the internal changes within me started to take place, I was prompted to begin writing about them because the feelings and emotions that began to occur in me were like nothing I had felt before. A blissful, joyous feeling was taking place inside me, which made me curious. I began to question what was really happening here.

This was the start of my awakening; I knew it was an awakening because I had gone through the same thing many years before, after the break-up with my first love, but didn't really understand what was taking place at the time. This time, however, was different – it was far more intense, and I wanted to know more, and to feel more. I wanted to know if other people were going through the same thing, and above all, why? Why would this happen to me? So, I began to research, and from my investigations I found that there was a lot of information available about emotional abuse, and plenty on the psychological aspects of it, but not much on the spiritual side of what was going on. Indeed, this is something that is not much talked about, so I took it into my own hands to speak about this. The research I did helped me to link the dots in my own life, and my intuition also played a part, being an excellent source of guidance. Today, I continue to develop my spiritual practice, and to make plans to include it in my life as much as possible.

In writing this book, I aim to share a piece of wisdom with others so that they are able to understand their own journey a little bit better. I look at this book as a source of loving counsel and if you come across it, then this is really no coincidence. It was meant for you, and I hope it will assist you to connect and make sense of the various facts and ideas that may have been going through your mind.

This book looks at what is going on in emotional abuse from a deeper, spiritual perspective. It explains why we may attract abusers, and examines what keeps us in such relationships, sometimes when every nerve in our body is screaming at us to get out. Yes, there are psychological issues aplenty, but this book explores the underlying 'why' of such issues and helps make sense of what can be a bewildering and confusing time in our lives. It looks at the possible role of karma and past life influences on our current relationships, and analyses why we may make soul contracts with certain individuals. The importance of transcending these contracts is also explored, and why the path of no contact is so vital if you are embroiled with a narcissist. As I said, this is a path of self-love, and so you will also find suggested ways to look after your healing and well-being, such as journaling, prayer and holistic therapies. Each chapter ends with a meditation and I invite you to take your time with these, and to relax and enjoy them so you gain the full benefit of what they have to offer. Above all I hope this book helps give meaning to suffering by viewing it as the necessary precursor to spiritual awakening and a richer, fuller life, filled with love and hope. Don't forget, though, that this book is only one link in your chain, and you can continue to source direction from your higher self.

Best wishes – I hope you enjoy and benefit from this book.

Paris xx
Email: stillhealing111@gmail.com
TikTok: @stillhealing111

Chapter 1

Healing

Healing is a big part of our lives. I believe that it's one of the main reasons why we come to Planet Earth and choose to experience being in a human body. We get to feel what it's like to have many different levels of emotions, with highs, lows and all that falls in between, all of which we need to know so that we can know life. And with this knowing comes spiritual growth. The majority of us are carrying some form of trauma, either from past lives or from our childhood. These wounds are what we seek to heal, both consciously and unconsciously.

Self-healing refers to the process of recovery. This process is usually inspired by our own instinct and requires some self-motivation, but can come about when we begin to notice that our own patterns are no longer serving our best interest. That instinct or gut feeling we have is a trusted source of guidance, which is telling us that change is needed. This is the first step in healing – acknowledging that something needs to change.

We then go through circles or patterns until change is made for our highest good. This can take months, years, our entire lifetime – or even two or three lifetimes, depending on how we apply ourselves and are able to adjust to the change. That being said, change is always certain as it is a natural part of life. What we are challenged with is trying either consciously or subconsciously to reach higher levels of soul growth. Sometimes life will push us to do this. So, sometimes change is forced upon us, meaning that we may not even know or expect that it is coming. Then, what we experience is there to give us a wake-up call, or to shift us in a different direction.

The people we meet, especially those with whom we form close relationships, tend to have a major impact on our lives and to play a big part in our development. From the moment we are born, relationships start to be made, from the midwife that delivered us, to our friends, family, teachers and everyone else in the equation – even someone that we meet at a bus stop and talk to for ten minutes before the bus arrives. All these people play a unique part in our story. For the most part we understand what the roles of these people are, such as our family, the doctor at the surgery, or our teacher at school. But the person at the bus stop – what about them? What do they do for us? Well, what they have to share with us may somehow facilitate us along our journey in some way, or lift our mood even if it's just for a short while. Or vice versa – we may have a tiny part to play in their lives without knowing it. We are all working together, giving or taking from one another, sharing our experiences, and all of it carries meaning.

The close romantic relationships we make regardless of the title. A partner, husband, wife, fling, long distance or open relationship. No matter what the status of the relationship, all of them are on our path for a very good reason, so we and the other person can experience all of the emotions that come with it and then go through a process of healing, either physically, emotionally or both. Sometimes we heal together as a couple and other times it's on our own. This all encourages us to reach a place of unconditional love, kindness, forgiveness and compassion for ourselves and others. This in turn leads to the higher levels of self-awareness and growth that we come into this life to experience. If the lesson is not learned in any given situation, then the process is repeated with a different partner.

For these challenges act as our teacher. We are the student, and Planet Earth is our school. No matter what age we are, there is always room for growth. If we didn't require any growth, we would not be having a human experience in the first place, and we would already have reached a place of higher consciousness and unconditional love for ourselves and for all human beings alike. That being said, some souls on earth have reached a place of enlightenment, and are here as helpers or healers, serving others who really need it. They could be your friend, mentor, or a complete stranger whom you encounter for a short period of time. These souls are aware of who they are, and in helping others they feel extremely satisfied, even if it means they get nothing in return. Being a supporter or healer in itself gives them much pleasure. While helping people who need it most, these souls tend to have jobs where they blend into society, getting by on minimal necessities, and requiring no credit for their work or for the support they give out freely and willingly.

The majority of us, however, need all the experience we can get, both positive and negative. In fact, experiences are neither good nor bad – it's only a matter of how we choose to categorise them. This is mainly due to the many years of earth programming we have received. Often, being told that something or someone is bad for us, we often accept this, and carry negative feelings towards them or a situation, when really everything is there to help us get to higher levels of understanding of our self and of others.

All of our experiences are there to help us reach our highest purpose – especially the ones we may perceive as negative or unfair. We have these challenges so that we can have appreciation and gratitude for what we already have in our lives. Challenges push us to further levels of development, showing us who we and others truly are – beings of love and light, our true nature. This is who we all are at a soul level.

The lows we go through are there to make us question our situation and find how best to deal with it so we can reach a solution. Eventually our pain triggers us into taking the required action, thus healing ourselves in one way or another. When we take responsibility for our healing, we are taking responsibility to support a part of the divine creation. This in turn creates a ripple effect that allows us to start supporting and helping others with their own healing. This again offers more healing for ourselves, and now we are creating a pleasant cycle, because supporting others to heal once we have healed ourselves offers a deeper level of heart cleansing.

True healing can only happen through unconditional love and forgiveness for ourselves and for others and this needs to be continually nurtured throughout our lifetime. We gain mental clarity from seeing how the challenges we face actively shape us and are the best source of growth. Although in the moment they may feel extremely painful, that pain will not last for ever because life is always changing and so are our feelings. Any pain we are experiencing is all a part of the transformation process.

Throughout this book I have included different types of meditation practices. Meditation is not related to any religious system, and involves more than becoming spiritually enlightened, vital though that is. It has proven value in everyday life and is known to improve an individual's mental and emotional health. The ancient art of stilling your mind aids in healing the body, mind and spirit, and so helps develop creativity and self-awareness. As you go through the chapters each meditation is like a stepping stone along your healing journey. I would suggest repeating each meditation for at least 21 days before moving on to the next. This way, the meditation has a chance to sink into your subconscious. However, it's entirely up to you. Do what works best for you – there is no right or wrong way to go about it.

Before beginning a meditation, though, it's important to set an intention each time. This way you are letting yourself and the universe know what you wish to achieve. It can be as simple as, 'I would like to open my heart to more love.' You can state your intention either out loud or in your mind. If you are new to meditation, setting an alarm can be a good idea so you don't need to focus your attention on the time. Find a comfortable space where you will not be disturbed, and enjoy some peace and quiet. However, you can also choose to meditate where and how you like – on the train or bus, if you have five spare minutes at work or are waiting in a queue, while walking, gardening or cooking – whatever works for you. It's important that you develop some peace of mind and mental space while dealing with the topic of our book, the narcissist.

Chapter 2

What is a narcissist?

I don't really like to use the word narcissist, because I believe that all of us can carry some of the traits I describe to one degree or another – although some more than others. But for easy reference, I will use the word 'narcissist' throughout this book to denote the person who, consciously or unconsciously, takes advantage of others, milks their good will and energy, and generally puts themselves first. This is in no way meant to offend anyone or to put down any person who believes he or she is narcissistic. It is simply for learning purposes, for healing, and in order to support both the abuser and the individual who is being or has been abused.

So, what is a narcissist?
A narcissist is one of several types of personality disorders. Narcissism can be defined as a mental condition in which the person has an inflated sense of their own importance or self, with a need for excessive attention and admiration from either one person or from many different people. Narcissists are described as having a lack of empathy, and sadly this often comes out in the form of abuse. It's likely that those who are closest to them, especially those in an intimate relationship with them, are the prime target of their abuse. This can be family, friends or a romantic partner.

Not every narcissist has been diagnosed with narcissistic personality disorder. Many of them slip under the radar and may appear to live a normal life. They are likely to be popular with many people outside their own circle – for example, their work colleagues will often find them extremely pleasant. It can be said that everyone in a narcissist's life gets to see a different version of them.

There may be a number of reasons why the majority of narcissists will not have had a full medical/mental diagnosis for their disorder from a professional. The individual may be unaware, meaning that they have not become self-aware as yet. They themselves may suspect that something is not right with their behaviour or emotions, but may not fully understand what it is. Then you have the narcissist who is aware but who may very well be in denial, not wanting to accept the truth or to take responsibility for their actions. They may also feel that there is no need for them to change, or that they shouldn't have to, because they feel as though they are always right and can't see any fault in their behaviour. This could be viewed as a defence mechanism. Narcissists may act superior to others, but they are actually deeply wounded individuals who are sensitive to criticism and fear embarrassment, especially public humiliation. Losing a partner's admiration is another major fear they tend to have and, when they sense this is happening, they will often generate jealousy, instil guilt or threaten to leave a partner.

Their behaviour is most usually a result of trauma during childhood. This could be from an upbringing that is generally lacking, or from receiving some kind of abuse themselves, be it sexual, emotional, physical or merely neglect. This abuse then creates a cycle, with the abused individual turning into an abuser. Some researchers suggest that narcissists have structural abnormalities in a region of the brain that is linked to low or no empathy for others, as a result of childhood trauma.

It would certainly appear that, because of the trauma, they are unable to process emotions the way that the rest of society does. An unhealed narcissist tends to offload their trauma – or, as I have heard it described, their 'toxic waste' – onto those who are closest to them in the form of abuse. The trauma they have faced is no excuse for their behaviour, but as you read on you will gain a deeper understanding of why encountering such a relationship, whether with a parent, friend or romantic partner, is no coincidence.

While some self-aware narcissists seek out professional help or use methods of self-healing, most don't. Many choose to live a lifestyle of inflicting pain onto others, hiding behind their own shame, despite the fact that the narcissistic abuser and the abused both are vulnerable individuals.

Some forms of narcissistic abuse can be difficult to detect, and many people who are suffering are not even aware themselves that they are being abused, or it may take many years before they realise something is not right. This is because narcissist behaviour may not be immediately obvious – for example, the person may start off using mean but subtle sniping or controlling comments here and there, that then escalate over time, and the abuse may not unfold until after many years. Anyone can become susceptible to being in an emotionally abusive relationship, mainly from a romantic partner, but it can also be from parents, friends, work colleagues or a manager. Those who have witnessed abuse at home or from previous partners are more likely not to recognise the behaviour as abuse, and therefore may find it more challenging to leave the situation as the behaviour is normalised by them.

The different types of narcissists

Here I am going to explain how to spot different types of narcissists. I want to stress that this is to educate and support others, and is in no way intended to put down or to judge anyone. Each and every one of us is still learning and growing as we walk our own unique path, and although some narcissists may be aware of their behaviour, change can only occur when they are faced with the truth, and then take responsibility for their behaviour. However, finding this truth requires going deep inside themselves, and understanding why they behave this way, it takes a great deal of self-reflection and a true desire to want to change.

As I have said, all narcissists are vulnerable individuals who need just as much healing as the people they abuse. I write about this abuse with the hope that we can have a more open, supportive and loving view towards narcissists. This may come as a shock to many people, but it is the best way to heal from any kind of abuse – with love rather than with hatred or anger. This is good for the narcissist because as we begin to become more aware of ourselves, and exercise our ability to take back our power, so abuse is less likely to take place. This can then have an effect on how the narcissist treats others in their life. In some cases, the actions of others trigger this change, and usually require stepping away from them, having respect for ourselves, and sticking by our morals and values.

In this chapter, I want to provide information about the different types of narcissists, and the labels put on them, from a scientific or psychological point of view. This isn't necessarily how I personally would view them – it is purely to help understand the kind of characteristics to look out for. In later chapters, I will explain the deeper spiritual meaning behind why this abuse occurs in our lives.

All narcissists want power at one level or another, and are driven by their own egotistical views, rather than by their higher selves. Many of them are successful in their careers, as they see this as a way of gaining power in the world. You may be wondering why it is that narcissists, being the way they are, tend to attract good karma in terms of their careers, and may be offered the highest, most trusted positions in a work setting. As I said above, many narcissists only reveal their full character to those closest to them, and so colleagues and acquaintances may be unaware of their abusive side. In addition, sad to say, their manipulative side and ambition may stand them in good stead when it comes to work values!

Attaining an authority role can also be explained in terms of the law of attraction. It's a common belief that the law of attraction stems purely from our thoughts. For example, positive thoughts will bring positive experiences, and negative thoughts will bring negative experiences. Simple, right? This, however, is not true. A person may think that they will be a millionaire for years and years, but it's likely that nothing will happen unless they take some kind of action towards gaining wealth. Positive thinking paves the way for this to happen – but is only the first step in activating the law of attraction. It's valuable because it is then likely to trigger someone into taking the next steps, such as setting up a plan, and then taking action to achieve the set goal. Now the law of attraction is in full motion. Wishful thinking alone is not enough.

In fact, the law of attraction does not understand positive, negative or ego – it only knows effect or action, meaning that if you are willing to apply yourself in a particular area, you will achieve your desired results. As the famous saying by Tony Robbins goes, 'Energy flows where attention goes.' Meaning, that what you put in is what you get back. Thus, many people in positions of power could be labelled as narcissistic – but the universe does not understand this, nor does it discriminate as to whether they are good or bad people. Atoms and energy do not judge who is good or bad, but follow spiritual laws. What the narcissist in power has done is to create a clear career plan and follow through on it, thus making their desires a reality.

The grandiose narcissist

This type of narcissist is one that is the easiest to spot. They usually have superficial charm, are attention-seekers and very bold, with a level of vanity that can often offend or embarrass others while they themselves have no shame in expressing it. They are very self-absorbed, with high levels of entitlement, often using this to exploit others, and having little or no care for the wishes or opinions of people. Some may be aggressive and possibly physically abusive. These people are assertive, overly confident and extraverted, having what could be described as an unrealistic sense of superiority and believing that they are too good for the average person. However, the grandiose narcissist is more likely to manage to maintain their relationships as they are adept at dominating people.

The vulnerable narcissist

Lesser obvious and not as well known is the vulnerable narcissist, also referred to as the covert or introverted narcissist. Like the grandiose type they too are self-absorbed, have a high sense of entitlement and may lack empathy either in general or just towards those whom they target for abuse. The vulnerable narcissist is usually shy, and fears criticism to a greater extent than their grandiose kin. These people experience low levels of self-esteem, anxiety, regret, and are generally unhappy with their lives. Their conflicted idea of themselves is unbalanced and goes back and forth from being inflated to negative, requiring continuous encouragement from others to keep their self-image high, and most often using manipulative tactics to achieve this. Unlike the grandiose narcissist, who feels confident, covert narcissists are likely to feel insecure, often resulting in a bitter approach to personal growth and distrust towards others. They are less likely to keep relationships, and their attachment style is usually avoidant.

The communal narcissist

Even more difficult to spot is the communal narcissist, a fairly new term. Like the grandiose type, they are outgoing but are likely to rate themselves using deliberate pro-social behaviour such as believing they are trustworthy and likeable with good social skills, able to work well with others, good at listening to others' problems and providing solutions. They rely on these communal aspects to satisfy their self-related needs and thrive on validation from society but, unlike the grandiose and vulnerable, are much better at not being recognised as a narcissist as they put hard work into their lives. However, they are still manipulative and tend not to emotionally invest in close relationships, but still appear to be helpful. The theory goes that the communal narcissist is only pretending to have others' best interests at heart, but that they do a very good job of pretending. They may seek approval, but, like the grandiose and vulnerable narcissists, they still want power. Communal narcissists tend to be popular as they say and do all the right things, making it even harder to spot them.

The malignant narcissist

This is considered the most dangerous type of narcissist. The malignant narcissist has many of the characteristics of the grandiose narcissist, but also can be cruel or even sadistic, taking pleasure in the pain of others and gaining a sense of power from making them sad or miserable. They have no remorse or guilt when it comes to mistreating others. They enjoy devaluing people, pointing out everyone's flaws. The malignant narcissist may spend a lot of time plotting, and will act with malicious intent. Not all narcissists are physically violent, but the malignant narcissist is likely to express violence, especially when they begin to view a person as their property. Their approach to life and love is cold. Purposely crushing a person's self-confidence and dominating them is no problem to them. Serial bullies, serial adulterers, gold diggers, rapists, child molesters and serial killers are all examples of malignant narcissists. The malignant narcissist is someone who needs professional and or spiritual support more than any of the other narcissistic types described, and is definitely the kind of individual you should avoid at all costs.

Chapter 3

Signs of a covert narcissist and how emotional abuse works

In this chapter I describe the red flags to look out for and how the danger signs can unfold in a relationship. Again, I would like to point out that this is to help others become aware of what they are facing, and is in no way designed to shame anyone, neither the abuser nor the abused. What I am exploring is how abuse is thought of in the world today, and how the cycles have played out for many people who have been a target for abuse. Although what I describe below can be the signs given off from any type of Narcissist, I have specifically chosen to write about the covert type, for two reasons. 1. It is believed that they are one of the hardest to spot; and 2. My Narcissist is a covert type or what I perhaps perceived.

From a psychological point of view, manipulation is a way that an individual can play mind games in order to seize power in a relationship, with the ultimate goal of controlling the other person to get what they want. This may be sexual favours, financial benefits – or just the desire to be in charge. This is often done in a sneaky manner, and can be difficult to spot as it is likely to be done slowly and to escalate gradually over time. The narcissist is often calculated in his or her actions.

At first, it may feel as though you have met someone who is just what you have been wanting from a partnership, taking the time to listen and let you speak about yourself first. Unfortunately, this may be viewed as a tactic they use. They may ask probing questions, encouraging you to share your thoughts and concerns early on, and reply by telling you all the things you want to hear, making their target feel very comfortable around them. They pay particularly close attention to any fears, insecurities or flaws their desired object shares, storing it up in their memory, so that they can use this later on in the relationship as 'a stick to beat you with' – that is, to put their target down or make them feel small about themselves. Conversely, the narcissist may open up about themselves very early on in the relationship, telling you their deepest secrets as a way of gaining your trust and tugging on your heartstrings.

Narcissists may have no problem in violating boundaries. They do this as a way of testing their target to see how far they can push them. For example, they may get very physical, overstepping the mark when you first meet, perhaps putting an arm round your waist. Or, they may gun for emotional closeness, demanding that you send them pictures of yourself. This can seem harmless at first but can escalate into nude pictures, and even if not, you have no control over where those pictures end up. (This also applies to pictures of your children which the narcissist may also ask you for 'out of interest' – beware, and treat any such requests with real caution.) Not only is this a way of testing you, but can also be a weapon for use later on in the relationship, even to blackmail you with if for example you decide you want to take action and expose the person, or to leave them. This effectively renders the abused person powerless, perhaps unable to tell anyone in fear that the narcissist will broadcast the pictures, or make out that you were the one harassing them, constantly messaging or emailing them. They may even ignore some of the pictures you send, as a form of mind control, so duping you into sending more pictures.

This narcissist wants to know how much of their behaviour they can get away with, and what you are willing to accept. Will you become angry, or get upset? Another way they test you is by feeding you lies about themselves or others to see how easily you believe them, and whether you take an objective viewpoint or challenge what they say. To them it's a game, and it's one they want to win. It's likely that at first you will not realise that you are playing a game. However, if you do get involved and play their game, you are also manipulating them, especially if you decide to pull away after getting to know them. This may seem confusing but I explain more in the chapter on empaths.

Narcissists often use a technique called gaslighting, where they rewrite the narrative and argue that theirs is the true version, even if you see or remember things differently. This is a manipulative type of behaviour and a form of mind control designed to undermine a person's entire perception of reality and to trick them into second-guessing themselves and their memories. Communicating with a narcissist who is gaslighting can leave you confused, dazed, questioning yourself and wondering what is wrong with you. You may end up afraid to trust your own experiences and memories of a situation. If a person continues to be gaslighted, it's likely to result in low self-esteem, creating a cycle that makes them even more dependent on the gaslighter for emotional support and validation. Over time, this can really affect an individual's confidence, especially in terms of knowing right from wrong, or reality from delusion. Gaslighting can be unintentional, and may happen in any relationship, usually to deflect responsibility for a mistake, or to cover up some kind of unsavoury behaviour such as an affair. However, when a narcissist does it, most often they are quite aware of what they are doing, and the gaslighting is intentionally done.

Some things to ask yourself are: Are you dealing with gaslighting? Or is it a completely different personality to your own? One that you may have never come across before, leading to miscommunication or seeing things from a different perspective.

Some of the signs to tell if it's really gaslighting:

- You get a strong gut feeling that something is not right, it's warning you.

- The gaslighting is repeatedly happening over time, as if they are purposely trying to put you down or trick you.
- They show no remorse or signs of internal struggle. If you do see either of these, then it is likely not gaslighting.
- They try to understand you and see things from your perspective. It's not always one-sided, they are interested in what you think.

Narcissists like to use the silent treatment as a method of punishment and control. They may keep a mental list of your faults and misdeeds, with a detailed memory for where they believe you hurt them, but, instead of confronting you and talking about what went wrong in a mature and open way, they use ignoring as a way of confusing you or making you feel guilty or not good enough. Instead of taking responsibility for their own actions, they put the blame on you. This is to cause a reaction from their target. However, it can also be a way of avoiding the situation, as this is how they process what has happened – indeed, it may be the only way they are able to manage what has happened. The abused person may have high levels of emotional intelligence, empathy, and skills in resolving conflict, and silence forces them to work diligently to respond.

The narcissist often uses the phone as a weapon in their game, as a method of controlling. Very often, emails, phone calls and text messages are not acknowledged by the narcissist, which can leave the abused person feeling upset and confused, perhaps desperately trying to get their attention and wondering what went wrong. With their lack of empathy, narcissists may go to the greater length of hanging up the phone on the individual while in conversation – an emotionally violent action which may cause a deeper wound and leave the target feeling shocked, causing further trauma bonding (when the abused person forms a deep attachment to their abuser, see below under *Stage 2 – Devaluation*).

Emotional abuse may involve loud, upsetting arguments, with no attempt to listen to or understand the other person, or to reach a compromise. The abuser may be offensive or threatening, often accusing the target of being needy or too sensitive.

Narcissists have a constant need for attention, which they may get from social media, where they may be very active, posting endless pictures of themselves. This may seem like the normal kind of thing that everyone does. However, individuals with narcissistic tendencies feed off the likes they get, and others' reactions boost their ego. They may have several social media accounts under many different names. This could be for different reasons, but one is to hide information from their main source of supply. When a narcissist doesn't get the reaction they desire, they may act out against their main source, posting offensive or defamatory content about them. Or, they may refuse to respond to your content, ignoring messages and giving you the silent treatment online, and sometimes even deleting photos they put up, say from WhatsApp or Facebook. This can be attention-seeking behaviour, because they won't or can't be direct in communication and in saying how they feel – you have to ask.

The three cycles of abuse in a partnership
Abuse works in cycles and will generally follow a pattern. This usually has a roller coaster effect and includes three stages:

Stage 1 – Idealization, valuation or honeymoon stage
A narcissist needs others to boost their ego and to feed their feelings of superiority, to affirm their grandiose fantasies, and to give them praise and admiration. The person or people they select is referred to as a source of supply. They often have a primary source, the individual who is closest to them, who is used and manipulated the most. They may also use different people for different reasons, for example one person could be used for sex while another for financial gain.

The narcissist often chooses someone who has low self-esteem, for example someone who they sense has already been abused, but they are also attracted to individuals who are successful, famous or hard-working. Anyone can be a target for them, in fact – it all depends on the narcissist's level of intelligence and what they are personally attracted to. So if you find yourself enmeshed with a narcissist, don't waste time blaming yourself – anyone can end up in a relationship with one. Narcissists like to put their targets in an 'eternal triangle' (known as triangulation) with another source of supply. This is done to keep the targets on their toes and make them jealous, a tactic that shows their low levels of empathy towards others.

During the first stage, the abuser will groom or 'love bomb' the abused person, showering them with attention, gifts and compliments, and putting them on a pedestal. Buying gifts and taking someone out on dates may sound harmless, but it depends on the level of control involved. In the narcissist's case, this is usually done with an agenda, to cultivate trust and commitment. This creates bonding and attachment, but they are also planting seeds of self-doubt which later result in emotional dependency as they gain power and control.

As well as investing in the person they want to keep in their life, in some cases the narcissist will talk big, telling them about all of the wonderful things they are going to do, such as fabulous holidays or expensive outings. They may even talk of marriage very early on. This again is to win the person's trust and can be false promises, with none of this ever happening. If it does take place, it's often with the motive of instilling obligations and creating the feeling that you now owe them something for all they have done.

Stage 2 – Devaluation

After a narcissist has completely hooked their target, they will start to become manipulative. The time it takes for the devaluation stage to begin varies from one relationship to another, meaning it could take weeks, months or even years. It will be subtle at first, and they may get family and friends involved. Or, they may try to isolate their target from loved ones. This a real red flag – by isolating you in this way, they stop you accessing support, which leaves you feeling divided and relying on the abuser and the abuser only for support.

Over time a narcissist will amp up their tactics, gaslighting even harder to deceive, twist, distort facts and lie. Some may become verbally abusive – they may insult, guilt-trip or blame you, or may shift or withhold money, love or permission to feel happy and safe. All of this is done to lower your self-esteem and to make themselves feel more powerful. Some narcissists can become aggressive and violent, again to push their target into becoming submissive. People receiving the abuse often feel the need to make excuses in order to justify the narcissist's behaviour. This is largely due to the first stage (idealization). Your mind keeps going back to those times of feeling loved by them, as is natural, and the narcissist will give you a little bit of love bombing here and there as well as the abuse, to keep you on your toes, confused and engaged. This is known as trauma bonding. Trauma bonding is when someone forms a strong connection with their abuser, and it comes from a cycle of devaluation and abuse punctuated by random positive reinforcement – the abuser hands out just enough love and respect to keep you hanging on. It's what makes a person stay in an abusive relationship and helps explain why it's often more complex than 'Just leave.'

When the abusive signs first come up, they are often dismissed by the target, as they feel a strong sense of loyalty towards the narcissist. Over time, as they become increasingly aware of feeling not good enough, the target may become increasingly confused and eventually start doubting their own sanity. They may end up longing for the person who once made them feel so happy, and may spend months if not years trying to get the narcissist back to the kind individual they once were, and hoping that their behaviour will change. This can be described as codependency (see below, *What is codependency?*).

Stage 3 – Discard

Narcissists have their own best interests at heart and are always on the lookout for what they can gain. They are often calculating in finding ways to get what they want, be it money, sex or the thrill of the chase at the beginning of a relationship. Once they have bled the target dry and exhausted all avenues, the mood changes, especially if they realise that you will no longer be providing them with the supply they need because you have worked out their game. Indeed, this may well become their new obsession, and they may target you as an enemy and act destructively towards you.

However, this is not always the case, and they may instead want to lure you in again, and to keep you in your old role of supplier to their needs. In some ways this is more disconcerting and confusing than outright rejection. Then the cycles may start all over again with what's known as 'hoovering' – attempts to draw you back into their lives (see below). Sadly, this isn't necessarily a sign that 'deep down, their intention is genuine'. By then, it's more likely that they view you as just another member of their entourage. If it was you who left the relationship then the narcissist would have sustained what is called a 'narcissistic injury' – the wounded ego they experience when they react negatively to the situation, or if boundaries are set with them or there are attempts to hold them accountable for their behaviour. The tables are turned, and their injured pride and self-worth may result in emotional trauma for the narcissist.

Note: When someone experiences feelings such as abandonment or shame, high beta waves may be generated in the brain. Beta waves are observed when the brain is awake and aroused, and are to do with mental activity. In emotional stress, the beta waves may respond to these negative feelings and shut down the area of the brain (the prefrontal cortex) that is responsible for rational thinking and decision making ('brain freeze'). In order to transcend these lower state thoughts and feelings, you want to stop living in the high beta brain waves of stress and live in the higher states of consciousness instead, which produce less stress, and this can be done through meditation. When you meditate, brain waves go into a delta frequency, which produces a calmer, more logical way of thinking in everyday life.

Narcissism terms

I've already used some of these terms, but here is a fuller explanation of what they mean.

What is the narcissist hoover?

This can be described as a type of emotional abuse or blackmail, and relates to how the narcissist will try and lure someone back into the relationship when he or she is looking to move away. The narcissist may use a variety of ways to appeal to your emotions and to rekindle the relationship, such as cries for help, loving words, romantic gestures such as gifts, or promises to change their behaviour. This is also a time where they may get their 'flying monkeys' involved – friends or family that they use to do their bidding. Flying monkeys is a term used to describe people whom the narcissist ropes in to act on their behalf, but they are not always aware of the web in which they are involved – bear in mind that, just as the narcissist manipulates you, so they manipulate others.

All of the above information has been gained from research into the phenomenon of narcissism. Many psychologists, doctors and other individuals have shared their knowledge of life with a narcissist, and have written about emotional abuse. If you have been a target of abuse and are reading this book, it's likely that you, too, have come across some of this information. It's a common theme that the narcissist is portrayed as an evil, egotistical individual whom we should all stay far away from for our own sanity and well-being. If you have been in a long-term situation with a narcissist, this is likely to be the most healthy answer. It's in your best interests – to keep away from them, begin healing and get on with your life. I will be exploring this in more detail later on in the book – it is called 'going no contact' with a narcissist.

The importance of energy

I do not find the narcissist's typical behaviour in any way acceptable, or view it as something that should be tolerated. However, it's important to realise that there is a reason why you will have had an encounter with this type of person, and it goes much deeper than you may believe. Modern society and statistics have created an inaccurate or limited definition of what narcissistic or verbal abuse is, based on psychology, but with little or no awareness of how energy works. Up until now, I have described narcissism and its components in conventional psychological terms, but I would like now to introduce you to the concept of energy and how we need to factor it in when considering narcissism.

There are different types of energy. Life force energy can be described as Qi, Chi or Prana, and is basically the same thing, depending on the belief system you follow. This is the non-physical force or aspect that exists in all living things and is meant to flow freely around the body. Spirit energy is the most subtle type of energy and has a close connection with our emotions. This type of energy is linked with our heart chakra and how we are feeling.

Words have power and can deplete our spirit energy. The energy of abusive words travels right through a person to the chakras, the seven main energy centres of the body. In energetic terms, this kind of force is just as strong as physical abuse, and therefore there is no verbal abuse without it also being physical on some level. Over time, it is likely that the effects of abuse will manifest in the body or mind, causing health problems, low self-esteem or depression. It is a scientific fact that what happens in the mind influences what happens in the body, and when we become agitated toxins are released from the glands and into the blood.

Doing some kind of spiritual practice like meditation can help you get rid of these poisons and bring back the natural flow to your body. I recommend that you practise the meditations at the end of each chapter to help restore physical balance and peace of mind.

Dantians – energy centres

The body has three main dantians – the lower dantian (located a few fingers below the navel); the middle dantian (located around the solar plexus); and the upper dantian (around the third eye area, between the eyes). A dantian is a storehouse of energy, whereas a chakra is a gateway. Dantians are associated with different vital energies, and it is important that, like our chakras, these energies remain balanced and unblocked.

The lower dantian is said to be the most important of the three, as it must be opened in order for the middle and upper dantian to be active. Our lower dantian is associated with the root and sacral chakras. When these chakras are balanced, the individual is able to have healthy relationships with themselves and with others, and they feel harmonious, content and nurturing.

Here is a technique that, when practised regularly, gives you the ability more freely to express your wants, needs and emotions, and to begin setting healthy boundaries with others. This technique can also be used to open the lower dantian and to activate kundalini energy.

- Find a quiet space where you will not be disturbed.
- Sit up as straight as you can while still feeling comfortable.
- Look straight in front of you, and focus gently on a spot on the wall.
- Gently stare at that spot until your eyes become heavy.
- When you feel ready, close your eyes and take a few deep breaths.
- Allow yourself to become relaxed.
- Place one of your hands just below the navel (use this as a point of focus for where you wish your breath to be guided to).
- Now with every in-breath, visualise the air you are breathing in as white light.
- See this air travelling down through your body, and entering into the space where your lower dantian is located.
- Imagine that the lower dantian is lighting up.
- Now with every out-breath, see this soft light from your lower dantian travelling back up through your body and exploding in your heart space.
- Continue to do this with every breath. Feel the lower dantian expand with beautiful light, cultivating energy in the lower dantian.

Continue to repeat this exercise daily for at least one week. After a week, you should aim to perform this meditation at least once a week to keep the lower dantian open.

Chapter 4

The empath and the super empath

In this chapter I will be discussing empaths, as these are the people who mainly tend to be in relationships with narcissists. This doesn't always apply – two narcissists can also be in a relationship together. This can be described as two superficial people attracting one another, as they both share similar values which draw them to each other.

In my opinion, as with the word narcissist, empath is another title that our ego mind uses to judge another individual or ourselves. Using the words narcissist and empath are our way of seeing something as either good or bad, right or wrong. But, these opposites are really two sides of the same coin. Our ego mind does one of two things: it can either give us a heightened sense of feeling superior, or it can trick us into believing we are not good enough. Either way, this is how the ego can deceive us, keeping us stuck in the illusion of separation and duality.

Existentially, nothing is contradictory, and everything is complementary to everything else. Contradictions are formed in the mind but in reality we are all the energy of divine oneness, although we forget this when we come to this earth realm. Really, at a fundamental level we are equal, and all of us require both some degree of narcissistic traits, and a level of empathy. It's about having a balance. Having the right skills at the right time in the appropriate situation is what will carry us in the world. For example, in a work setting, a manager's role is to control work flow and performance. She may come across as displaying narcissistic behaviours in order to show authority, but at home this manager is also a mother who is highly empathic towards her children. Having healthy narcissism is something we all can use, because it is healthy self-esteem. This is what makes us

31

pick ourselves up after failure, and to keep going with our lives. It also gives us the ability to love someone, because we already know how to love ourselves in a healthy way.

Like all opposites, both sexes have masculine and feminine energy. If you are a female in this lifetime, it's likely that your female energy is more present as this is your signature side, and vice versa if you are residing in a male body. If you have been involved with a narcissist long-term, then your feminine energy is more dominant. The feminine energy is heart centred and is the essence of compassion and empathy, while masculine energy is about logic, thinking, decisiveness and having boundaries. Female energy craves for unity and togetherness. It is a powerful energy that holds the vibration of unity consciousness, but if this is not balanced with masculine energy an individual can become lost, giving too much of themselves. Masculine energy ensures that a person stays centred and has good boundaries, and can let others go at the appropriate time.

It's important to make conscious use of both energies, masculine and feminine, as this brings about a harmonious, balanced individual. Currently the masculine brain tends to dominate much of the world, although this is slowly changing as we enter into a new era of heart-based consciousness. The overriding emphasis on rational thought on everything it sees, hears or experiences is now being challenged with the feminine brain, an energy guided by our intuition and feelings. Having boundaries and embracing our masculine side, our energy reflects self-love, and this is how we can correct narcissist behaviour without actually doing anything.

Going back to empaths, to have empathy means being able to place yourself in someone else's shoes and feel what they are feeling. The word empath, when applied to another person, is just a label, and labels create separation. Separation is needed for understanding, just like the labels and titles we use.

However, at our core we are all the same energy, divine love, and light, and separation does not exist – it is something that our mind makes up. It is nothing but an illusion, perceived via the frequency of the third dimension – an illusion that cuts us off from our true spiritual self.

Although we are all love and light, at a core level all of us still carry dark energy within us. However, this is in no way a negative thing. The darkness helps to balance us, something we need in order to make us whole, and to understand life. Growing up, many of us tend to explore life before settling into adulthood. Some people experiment with drugs, question their sexuality, or may even do things that they later regret.

If this applies to you, there is no need for you to carry any harsh emotions with you for the rest of your life. Whatever happened was meant to happen, and all of it was a learning experience for you and for anyone else involved. It all took place to help everyone know who they are, and to choose what part of themselves is going to dominate, the positive side or the negative side.

What felt good and what felt not so good, what was safe and what was dangerous – exploring your dark side is a positive thing when it comes to growth. All of these experiences are needed to gain understanding of who you are, and indeed most often, it helps to shape who you are, teaching you right from wrong and what is the best route for you. There is honestly no wrong or right answer to the path you choose. It's up you and what feels right for you. It's all needed to create a balance in the world, and whatever you decide, it all plays a part in the divine creation and human experience, a balance of all. Positive and negative, dark and light, yin and yang, masculine and feminine. All of it is needed and has its place in the universe, working simultaneously together, creating oneness. It's your choice what path you decide, and what energy is going to have a greater influence over you.

The more evolved your soul, the more likely it will be that you will gravitate towards the light, gravitate towards a human experience that is based on the highest good. Many people, narcissists included, are still evolving and are not at a place of all knowing and complete love. They may therefore choose to operate from a lower state rather than from a higher self, continuing to seek out short-lived, quick gratification-based experiences. However, through these experiences they are moved towards a greater knowing of self-love.

As with the word narcissist, I will be using the words empath and super empath, but this is in no way intended to judge anyone. It is purely for the purposes of understanding, supporting others to reach higher levels of growth and self-awareness. These are only labels and no one is better than anyone. We are all evolving at our own personal rate, and each and every one of us has an important role to play in the grand game of life. Many empaths who end up in relationships with narcissists had a parent who displayed narcissistic tendencies, and abuse usually starts in the home, with the person being abused as a child, or seeing one parent abuse another. The person may have grown up thinking that this behaviour is totally normal – why wouldn't they, if that is all they have known? This naturally makes them more susceptible to such behaviour in adult life, resulting in them being overly compassionate, or too giving to others, with limited boundaries. However, conversely, a child who witnessed narcissistic abuse, instead of being highly empathic, may also grow up to display narcissistic tendencies. Either way, one thing that both narcissists and empaths have in common is that they are both highly sensitive people.

Everyone is born with a degree of empathy. Life situations and upbringing play a part in how it develops, and everyone can develop the skill of empathy with practice; therefore, empathy is both a skill and a trait. It's within our close relationships that we tend to build this skill. Compassion and understanding

how others feel play a crucial part in sustaining the future of
humankind and how we evolve.

The empath

As I mentioned above, empaths are highly sensitive people,
who are able to pick up on or sense what the people around
them are thinking or feeling. In energetic terms, it is believed
that empaths can absorb positive and negative energy just by
being in someone's presence. Some empaths find crowded
places overwhelming, and many of them feel more comfortable
being on their own or in small groups of people.

Empaths can also be more sensitive to sounds. Certain sounds
may trigger an emotional response in them, and they may also
prefer to listen to music or watch television at low levels. Some
empaths have psychic abilities known as clairsentience, which
can be defined as having a clear feeling. This makes it easy for
them to sense other people's emotions and to analyse these
emotions at depth. In some cases, empaths are more vulnerable
to manipulation, due to their strong desire to help others,
and to their readiness to overlook negative behaviour. A deep
understanding of pain and a compassionate nature are what can
lead to them being used and abused by a narcissist.

Signs of empathy

- Empaths tend unconsciously to mirror another person's
  emotions. Some researchers believe that mirror neurons
  fire in the brain in some forms of empathy, making us
  more able to feel what the other person is feeling.
- Empaths find crowded or busy places like shopping malls
  difficult or unbearable.
- They are less likely to display aggression, and are more
  likely to have a calm approach to life.
- Empaths are quicker and more accurate at recognising
  emotions, usually from another person's facial expressions.

- Fragrances and odours may affect them more strongly.
- Certain sounds may trigger an emotional response.
- Empaths may be more vulnerable to manipulation or to toxic behaviour, as they have a deeper understanding of others' pain and know how to be supportive.
- They have good intuition skills – they can often sense what is going on without being told.

Because they can read others' reactions, empaths are more likely to try new things in life such as food or activities – if they see someone is enjoying something, they will feel encouraged to join in as well. However, despite being highly attuned to the feelings of others, some empaths find it difficult to relate to people because they find it so draining. Others may not understand why they become exhausted and stressed out so quickly after spending time in company.

People with empathy have the ability to promote a more harmonious community, and tend to be the mediator among their family and friends who helps reduce others' stress or aggression. They are good at maintaining social bonds and at supporting others in maintaining those bonds. Because they feel and understand people so well, empaths want to help people who are experiencing difficulties.

They tend to be generous and frequently give to charities or to homeless people on the street. This is a gesture that often comes from their heart space – as I explained, we are all working simultaneously together, and empaths feel this deeply. Giving a homeless man or woman some food or spare change is also beneficial for the empath, because they are creating a pleasant feeling within the homeless person. This vibration of positive energy is then returned and transported back to the empath's aura, creating good karma for them. Their acts of kindness are most often repaid in the most unexpected ways, but usually just the act of helping someone gives them compassion satisfaction and they do not require anything in return. This can also be explained by the cosmic law of give and take, which states that the universe operates through this dynamic exchange. Giving and receiving are different aspects of the flow of energy in the universe, and you must give and receive in order to keep wealth and abundance circulating in your life.

Super empaths hold all of the same qualities as an empath. However, they tend to have a deeper intuition about what the people around them think and feel. They have strong self-awareness and are often the ones who remain calmer in a room of talkative people – they like to be the observer, and this is something that comes naturally to them. Often, they may come across as reserved, quiet, and even cold, in manner, keeping others at a distance and not giving their trust easily. Super empaths often have a high level of emotional intelligence and know how to set clear, healthy boundaries with others.

Some empaths have what can be described as sensory overload. This is when their environment around them literally becomes 'too much' – their brain becomes overwhelmed by the stimuli to their five senses of sight, hearing, smell, touch, and taste, and is unable to process the information. For example, being talked to incessantly, or being touched, can be too much for some people, although their need to break away and have alone time can sometimes offend others who don't understand. Then of course the super empath absorbs the feelings of those they have offended, which brings them even more distress.

Empaths on the whole are rarely physically confrontational. They are tactical and have the ability to soak up a lot of abuse, either ignoring it or brushing it off until things reach a breaking point. When this happens, the empath often 'goes supernova', or in other words, behaves like a star that is exploding! This is a term used when the empath is triggered by too much stress either on the psyche or the soul, which triggers a reaction in the empath so that they themselves take on narcissistic traits as a self-protective measure.

Super empaths tend to reach breaking point a lot quicker, and usually do not end up in a long-term relationship with a narcissist, as their sensitive nature finds it too much to handle. The abuse tends to send their body into a state of shock (the awakening) and they will most likely leave before the narcissist even gets a chance to discard them. The whole thing is far too exhausting for them. They absorb the energy of the world around them, which is challenging, and can leave them totally burnt out.

Empaths are gifted with a great deal of compassion for others and have the ability and strength to withstand the abuse for long periods of time – many months or even years. They try many different ways to make the narcissist change, due to their deep care and need to help others. Empaths experience spiritual awakenings, but most often this is after the relationship has ended and they have stepped away from the narcissist. Awakenings tend to occur much quicker for some empaths, especially once the devaluation stage has started. They know something is not right, but they can't put their finger on it, and the super empath in particular will go along with it for a while, not putting up a fight. But not for very long – pretty soon, something inside them changes, like a light switch turning on. Reality kicks in and they will start to see the narcissist and the abuse for what it really is – they will then walk away and let it go, and move on with their lives.

Some empaths may seek to destroy the narcissist's ego. They can't understand how someone can be this way, and may spend years of their life trying to fix it. Feelings of resentment and bitterness can arise, and they may act on these (in vain, be it said). On the whole, though, they see the positive traits in a narcissist, and instead of taking revenge, they just want to get that good person back, the one whom they first met.

What is codependency?

This is a bit of a risky term to use, in that it is used pretty casually nowadays to describe how dependent one person is on another; however, for the purposes of information I decided to add a section about codependency because it has particular relevance to narcissism. To get a fuller picture, this is more than just relying on your partner. A codependent person will plan their entire life around pleasing another person. This is often the story for the narcissist and empath relationship. Codependents have a degree of empathy, although not all empaths are codependent.

From my findings, the codependent is often described as an enabler by many doctors or psychologists, in the case of the narcissist and empath relationship. That is, a codependent empath will enable the person to continue with their patterns of abusive behaviour. This can be viewed as unintentional manipulation. Therefore, both individuals are feeding off each other's low vibration, and while people usually view the narcissist as using their supply to fulfil their own grandiose needs, it can work both ways. Both are actually using one another. In the case of a codependent, they rely on one person – the narcissist to fulfil all their emotional and self-esteem needs, whereas a narcissist may rely on several people.

The difference between a codependent and an empath is that codependents have a harder time creating boundaries, in some cases. They have a harder time saying no, and, because of their compassionate nature, feel responsible for people's problems to the extent where they may put others before themselves and may even feel hurt and rejected if told their help is not required. This is when caretaking or people-pleasing can be used as a form of manipulation, although a codependent may not be fully aware of this. In their eyes, they are being supportive and want to help their partner or loved one in any way they can, even if that means putting their own needs aside. For some people, however, this may be their only way of understanding how to control a situation.

Individuals who are in abusive relationships may be aware that something is wrong. However, there is an external push to make a relationship work and an internal battle to leave. There is so much emotion involved and so many decisions to face. It is totally up to the individual, and I personally do not judge anyone who does not feel that they are in a place to leave. If you do want to take yourself out of a codependent situation, everything has to be carefully weighed up and thought through before making the move. Life is continuously throwing obstacles at us. But that doesn't mean we can't successfully dodge them. If you do decide to leave, make sure that plenty of support is available, and do not fear because, as the saying goes, when a door shuts a window opens.

Below I have created a meditation for codependents. This is a loving heart chakra meditation, to help uplift any divine souls struggling with codependency. This is nothing to be ashamed of. It is purely a sign of someone who has so much love to give and who wants to be loved in return, but has blemished programming that often stems from childhood wounds, resulting in feeling unlovable or rejected. You may feel it is not safe for you to express your own desires and needs, in which case I do encourage you to try meditating. This meditation is filled with mantras and will guide you in tuning into your highest vibration. Repeating mantras out loud, in your head, or by writing them down can aid in correcting any faulty programming that you may have absorbed as a child. This meditation supports you in becoming your whole healthy self by reversing any negative thought patterns and replacing them with constructive ones.

Meditation technique for releasing feelings of codependency
- Find a comfortable space where you will not be disturbed for at least 15 minutes.
- If you want, you can play some heart chakra meditation music or binaural beats to help you relax.

- Lie down or sit up in a chair, ensuring your spine is straight.
- Breathe in deeply through your nose and hold for three seconds, then release and let it out your mouth. Do this at least ten times.
- At this point you may close your eyes.
- When you are ready, breathe normally.

Now say these words either out loud or in your head:

- I love myself and I deeply accept myself.
- I am safe and it is safe for me to relax.
- I am a loveable, divine being.
- I am perfect just the way I am.
- People love me, people absolutely love me.
- The universe has so much love to give me.
- And I open myself up to receive all the love from the universe.
- I ask that my higher self comes and joins me.
- If you have not already closed your eyes, you can do this now. Breathe in deeply through your nose a few more times, holding each breath for three seconds, then release through your mouth.
- Now imagine that the top of your head is opening up.
- See a beautiful white light coming from the sky.
- This light enters into your head through your crown chakra.
- The light travels down through your body, filling you with warm, loving energy.
- Feel this light energy expanding in your body.
- Now imagine that the vortices on the soles of your feet are opening up.
- See beautiful white light coming from the earth and travelling in through your feet and up your body.

- With this light beaming through your body, see as it travels up to your heart space. This light penetrates into your heart, illuminating your heart chakra.
- Visualise and feel the white light expanding all around your chest area.
- Now repeat these words five times:
  - I love myself and I love others.
  - I have healthy boundaries.
  - I know when to say no and I know when to say yes.
- When you are ready open your eyes and thank your higher self for the experience.
- Continue to repeat this exercise daily for at least a month.

Chapter 5

Going no contact

Making the decision to step away from a narcissist can be difficult, regardless of if you made the decision yourself, or you were discarded. Letting go of anyone with whom we have formed a close bond is not easy, even though we may be feeling confused, hurt or let down, and knowing that we gave our trust and put so much effort into making it work. It's likely that this process of letting go will take some time. As with any break-up, time to heal is needed, but with an abusive relationship it may take longer. If this sounds like you, remember to be patient with yourself. You may have to go through many cycles before you finally let go. Research suggests that people who are in an abusive relationship go through approximately six to eight cycles before they are truly able to let go. In some cases if a person feels a strong desire to go back this is the voice of their soul letting them know that another cycle needs to plays out, that will bring a new level of awakening. The length of the cycle varies from one individual to another – it could be weeks, months, or it could be years. Some choose to stay for their entire life. Either way go easy on yourself and remember you are not alone. The length of time you choose to stay for is relevant for your own unique development, and your soul sends you intuitive feelings when it is time to shift again.

You may have put all your hope into thinking that a person can change, but the truth is that we are who need to change. We need to change our thinking and to really understand our self-worth, along with developing self-care, self-awareness and tolerance. Having a firm set of morals and values in place is something that often develops with life experience. Changing is not always easy – it takes courage, strength and the wisdom to know your true worth. Trying to change another person should not be a priority. Instead, direct your attention to yourself.

Throughout this book I use the word cycles. This refers to a process that is relevant to every aspect of life. Everything works in cycles; nothing stays the same, and life itself is a cycle. A day is a cycle, a week is a cycle, the moon has a cycle, we work a job for a cycle. If you think about your life, it is all based around cycles and if you believe that you are an eternal being, then you understand that death is the ending of one cycle and the start of another.

The term no contact literally means having no contact at all with the narcissist – therefore no staying friends, no accepting gifts from them, no taking their phone calls, no emails or following them on social media. No contact means completely cutting them off. Cutting them off physically is not enough. You have to release them emotionally and spiritually, meaning no more fixating on them in any way. This can take some time, depending on how long they were in your life and/or the effect they had on you. Some people describe narcissists as energy vampires (someone who depletes all your energy), but what is really happening here is that if you knowingly, unknowingly, consciously or unconsciously play power games with another person, hooks attach to your auric field. This results in tears (as in rips or damage), leaks and blockages in the different layers of the aura. When this happens, and you separate from a narcissist and go no contact, it can feel like your energy is being leached out of you. Meditating and using affirmations will assist in pulling your energy back to you.

Be easy on yourself. Some days you may find that you are overly obsessing, while others not so much. The cycles need to play out. At some point you may feel that you have really let go, only to find that the next day all those feelings come flooding back. This is all normal, and it does get easier. What you are experiencing is the detox phase. This often comes with a feeling of emptiness and with massive cravings for the person who is no longer in your life. As with any detox, you go through a withdrawal period. I cannot say how long this period lasts. It all depends on the individual; every relationship is different, and while there may be some similarities between everyone who goes through a break-up with a narcissist, no two experiences are the same.

No contact is needed because a narcissist will often leave the door open, meaning they will not give you any real closure. (See my reference to hoovering above, the process whereby a narcissist will try and pull you back in if you seek to distance yourself.) Some narcissists will go to the extent of increasing the abuse in order to push you away so that you break up with them. This allows them to keep the power and stay in control. Often, they are aware of their behaviour. Their tactics may be deliberately used to keep you coming back, keeping you on a string, shifting the blame and having you believe it's all your fault. Narcissists like to paint themselves in a positive light, especially to your friends and family.

It's up to you to break these cycles or patterns, and you will know within yourself when that time is right for you. Do not blame yourself. Narcissistic behaviour, like codependency, stems from faulty programming, be it from society, culture, family, general life experiences or even past life trauma. For example, they may perhaps have had a previous life where they were extremely compassionate, but this compassion was not truly reciprocated. This does not excuse their behaviour, but may help you understand why they act the way they do. A narcissist, whether male or female by gender, is dominated by their masculine energy, although in a low vibrational way. Healthy masculine energy knows how to have boundaries with others but does not seek to control or take pleasure in mistreating another person. Generally speaking, a narcissist has a different way of expressing their feminine energy, the side that is responsible for matters of the heart like compassion and empathy. Having the right amount of these energies in any individual supports a healthy way of giving and receiving in all relationships, ensuring that one person is not exploited while the other takes and takes.

For your safety it is extremely important to ensure that you have support around you from friends, family or professionals before going no contact. Only leave the situation when you are sure that you will be safe in doing so. Statistics show that leaving an abusive individual can be the most dangerous time for the person who is being abused, and the risk of homicide increases at this point. Not all, but some narcissists will resort to becoming aggressive or violent if they become aware you are planning to leave them. You don't want to put yourself in any danger, and if you feel in any way unsafe, scared or threatened, it's important that you trust your instincts. In this case, leaving a narcissist should be carefully planned out and done in steps. Seek professional help and advice from your GP, social services, the police or charities that specialise in domestic abuse, and use their support if need be to help ensure your safety.

If you have children with a narcissist, then you may not be able to completely go no contact. In this case, you may want to get advice on how best to manage the situation and plan a strategy. You may be advised to use the grey rock method. This basically means you become emotionally non-responsive and communicate in a boring way – you virtually act like a rock. Because manipulative people tend to feed off drama, the grey rock method ensures that you offer them nothing to get hold of, so that the conversation cannot escalate. This emotional detachment serves to undermine a narcissist's attempt to manipulate you or to pull you back into their life. Applying this method is up to you. Many professionals would advise it, although I believe that it depends on your own unique situation and the length of time you have spent in the relationship. If it was long-term, this method may be a good option for you, especially in the beginning when you decide to part ways. The more time you have apart, the more you may naturally find that your feelings are no longer the same for them as they once were. This healing offers you tremendous strength and you begin to value yourself, knowing that no one should seek to use another human being for their own egotistical needs.

However, it's important that you take responsibility for your part in the relationship, as this aids with your healing. By taking responsibility, I mean understanding that your emotions are your own and no one else's. It is within your power to change any negative feelings – this can take some practice, but it is most definitely achievable. It's all about rewiring your mind into a higher vibration. By sticking around the narcissist, you are not helping either yourself or them to change – this has to happen apart from one another. It's important for you to focus on your own healing, and not that of the narcissist. It's up to them to desire change for themselves, and it is not for you to do anything apart from concentrating on your own life. We all have free will and our own choices to make, and we certainly can't make those choices for others, however much we may feel the urge to help.

If you have children with a narcissist, then applying the grey rock method is usually advisable. How the contact goes between the children and the narcissistic parent is up to you all to decide. It all depends on your own unique situation, and what the parenting skills of the narcissist are like. Do you feel that the children are safe with him/her? Are they reliable? Are they respectful towards the children? These are some of the questions you need to ask yourself before making a decision. If you need it, there are many options and support available to you, such as therapy, group support and charities. If you are unable to come to an agreement with your narcissist, legal aid can help things to go smoothly. I suggest you have a lawyer at hand just in case.

Once no contact begins, many people experience urges to go back to the narcissist. Taking back your power (energy) often comes with an unexpected struggle that can last weeks, months or years. This is because, usually with a narcissist, it is not an everyday connection – it's a spiritual one, or a soul tie. It can literally feel as though your soul or a massive part of you is tied to the other person. When two people play power games with one another, a cord of attachment is formed between them both. Sometimes, this tie is already there from a past life.

Long-term narcissistic abuse can have effects on the brain. Studies suggest that traumatic stress can have an impact on the brain regions known as the amygdala, hippocampus, and prefrontal cortex, affecting functions such as memory, concentration, and decision-making, along with anxiety and mood.

In the spiritual world these side effects are described as black magic. They can also be viewed in terms of a physiological addiction to the narcissist. This type of stress can be more challenging for some than others. If you have been subjected to this abuse either long or short-term, depending on your situation it can lead to post-traumatic stress disorder (PTSD). The strain of the connection can put your body under enormous stress resulting in PTSD-type symptoms such as flashbacks, headaches, insomnia and depression. Chronic stress can also promote inflammation in the body, leading to a range of physical problems from digestive upsets and a weakened immune system to high blood pressure and other problems with heart health – even death from a stroke or heart attack, if it's too much to bear.

PTSD also occurs when you step away from the person. This is because the brain has rewired itself and has become used to the roller coaster effect of living with an abusive person, so that the comedown can leave some individuals feeling extremely withdrawn from their environment and from the people around them. Persistent feelings of fear and worry can creep in, especially if they don't know what to expect from the narcissist in terms of behaviour. This can trigger anxiety and depression. If this happens, it's important to allow yourself to experience the discomfort and let yourself grieve. Depression is a spiritual disorder but along with it come physical symptoms such as lack of energy, loss of motivation, insomnia, panic attacks and finding it hard to take care of yourself, to name a few, so if you need to, do consult your doctor about your symptoms.

After you decide to go no contact, you may find yourself experiencing mental conversations with the person. What I mean by this is, communicating with them in your head, or having an internal dialogue with them. This is part of the addiction to the narcissist. At first you may try and normalise or deny things, a mechanism which acts as a kind of comfort blanket and makes it much easier to live with. Gradually, as the shock of everything sets in, feelings of anger, resentment and confusion arise, mixed with the urge to talk to the person and state your side of the story loud and clear. This is what usually prompts these 'head conversations', which can last for months or even for years. At the end of this chapter, I have created a meditative practice to support people with mental conversations and obsessive thinking. I hope you will find it helpful.

If the abuse was severe and/or lasted years, the trauma of the experience or the shock of abandonment and rejection can cause some people to feel suicidal. If this is the case for you, it's critical that you speak to someone if you are having suicidal thoughts. This is not an uncommon way to feel, indeed, many people go through this. It is a natural result of the deep attachment you have to the narcissist. You are not alone. This path can be a difficult one. However, there is light at the end of the tunnel, which leads to deeper healing, higher self-worth and increased self-love – all of which I will be exploring in later chapters. Painful and frightening though suicidal thoughts may be, experiencing them often paves the way for growth and healing. A term that was developed in the early 1990s is 'post-traumatic growth' (PTG), which is also experienced after a break-up with a narcissist and forms another phase of your awakening process. I will explain the awakening in more detail later (see Chapter 6, Spiritual awakening).

Smear campaigns

Depending on your relationship, the narcissist may start a smear campaign against you. This is when they get other people involved, who know you both, and try and convince them that you have done something wrong, or that the failure of the relationship was all your fault. There may be an element of truth to what they are saying – for example, that you abandoned the relationship – but expect this truth to be manipulated. No way will the narcissist explain truthfully just why you left the relationship. They may put effort into co-opting others to his or her side. They may tell blatant lies about you and take on the role of a victim, telling friends and family how crazy, manipulative and unbalanced you are, because they want to maintain their image of perfection and to keep earning admiration from others.

You may be tempted to strike back at them. However, it's important not to engage in the battle, as their behaviour may escalate, resulting in them openly directing their rage towards you with insults and threats. Remember, they are still seeking control over you. Be the bigger person and walk away. They want you to play their game. If you play it with them and seek to win, or to take some kind of revenge, you are lowering yourself to their vibration. Healing yourself is what is important and you need space to do this. You must put yourself first.

If you have to go through a smear campaign, remember, it can only affect you if you allow it to do so. Healing involves learning to love yourself above anyone else, and to ignore their opinions. Yes, it can hurt, but learning not to care about what others think is key. Don't get caught up in their drama. If others want to join in with their hate campaign, walk away, and remind yourself you are kind and loving and that you deserve respect. There is no need to defend yourself. It's likely that during the relationship you would have had to do this several times – why continue, and now explain yourself to others? This is only a trap the narcissist uses to control your emotions and to drain your energy. They want you to react; instead stay calm, stoic and uninvolved. You may be able to prevent some damage by telling your own family or mutual friends what is happening and letting them know that you are the target of a smear campaign. State your side of the story once, then let it go. Don't spend time trying to convince others of the truth.

Cutting energy cords

Some individuals recommend a spiritual procedure known as cutting the energetic cord with a narcissist. The idea behind this is that, when you bond deeply with someone, a cord made of energy connects the two of you. These invisible cords link each other's energy bodies or fields, and keep the energy flowing between you. A pregnant mother is linked to her child via the umbilical cord, and while this is cut when the child is born, there is still an energy cord connecting mother and child. Other energy cords are formed from intimate relationships, be it sexual, emotional or both. The deeper the connection between two people, the thicker and stronger the cord will be.

A connection with a narcissist is often strong and is very likely to be draining. This is because one person (the narcissist) takes the energy, and the other person gives. This happens either unconsciously or consciously. Energy cords make us feel closer to the person but sometimes it can feel as if we are too close. I expect you have felt this yourself with your narcissist, even if perhaps you've been unable to explain why. There is literally a 'special bond' between the two of you, and this is partly what fools you into thinking that you have an exceptionally close and special relationship.

Once you become aware of the cord, you can usually feel it. I don't actually advise cord cutting in this case – instead, I would recommend pulling your energy back to you. Cord cutting can work if practised repeatedly – however, it does not deal with the root of the cord, meaning that your attachment to the person can come back because the energetic connection is still there. Cords are formed for a reason and may even extend back to a previous life you have shared with an individual, in which case karma may be at work. It's important that you heal that karma first, and this can take some time, but meanwhile, pulling back your energy will help you to become grounded and to re-energise yourself back to wholeness.

Below I have created a meditation that focuses on pulling your energy back. This is a form of distance healing that enables you to connect with anyone you feel you have given your power away to.

- Find a comfortable space where you will not be disturbed for at least 20 minutes.
- Sit up or lie down – just ensure that your spine is straight.
- Breathe in deeply, through your nose and out of your mouth.
- Allow yourself some time to become relaxed.
- Now repeat these words out loud or in your mind:
  - 'All energy that I have given away, I ask to return back to me.'
  - 'All energy known and unknown that has been scattered near and far, I ask that it returns back to me.'

- ○ 'I cleanse my energy with light and love and I let go of any fears that are blocking me from moving forward.'
- Now close your eyes and imagine a glowing ball of energy above the top of your head, where your crown chakra is. See all of your scattered energy being sucked back into the glowing ball.
- See the energy appearing as waves of light, flowing back into the energy ball above your head.
- Take a moment and concentrate on your breathing.
- See the glowing energy ball travel down through your crown chakra and into your head.
- Imagine the energy spreading throughout your whole body.
- Feel the energy travelling down your neck, down each arm, into your core, then down your legs.
- Say to yourself, 'I accept all my energy back.'
- And when you feel ready, open your eyes.

Repeat this meditation daily for 21 days.

Chapter 6

Spiritual awakening

Many individuals who share a bond with a narcissist, or who experience emotional abuse, tend to go through a spiritual awakening at some point, usually after the relationship ends or they step away from the person who is abusing them. Because an awakening is different for every individual, it can't be specifically defined, but in simple terms it can be described as a new-found awareness of a spiritual reality, during which the dimensions of reality beyond the ego mind begin to dissolve and let go, allowing room for our higher self to step in. All of us have an ego, and it is needed to balance our moral and idealistic standards. However, it's important not to allow the ego to dominate us, as this involves the lower aspect of our spiritual self.

When we leave the spiritual realm before a new incarnation on earth, we leave behind our real selves of pure love and light, our memory is wiped clear, and ego becomes present. An awakening occurs to remind us of who we really are, and through the stages gradual conscious awareness is received. Many individuals experience an awakening during or after trauma of some kind. A traumatic experience tends to change us, and questions will often pop up. Why has this happened to me? How could this happen to me? What we are doing here is reflecting on life, which then opens up doors within us, doors we have never opened before, to places we didn't quite understand. These feelings tend to challenge our belief systems and habits. After such traumatic experiences as the break-up of an abusive relationship, physical injury, or losing a loved one, our heart opens up, pushing aside the ego and, very often, activating an awakening.

This can be described as a heart chakra awakening, or kundalini awakening. Kundalini may be understood as an internal force, that helps us to navigate and align with our true self, the higher self. Kundalini energy helps heal the internal wounds in our physical, emotional, mental and spiritual body, by encouraging us to release all the behavioural patterns that do not serve us on our path to enlightenment or self-development. Kundalini awakening practice aims to cleanse our chakra system, so that the energy of spirit can flow easily through us. Some individuals activate a kundalini awakening through practising meditation. If your awakening is activated by trauma of some kind you may wish to seek out help from a realisable spiritual healer as it can trigger uneasy feelings. This is of course entirely up to you.

Before an awakening

Naturally, as human beings we are drawn to wanting the best for ourselves, and once we achieve one goal, we tend to set out another and to begin a new cycle, craving more and more of whatever it is that drives us. Acting on our desires is what often leads to a spiritual awakening, and indeed I believe it is divinely crafted in this way to give us the maximum benefit. We in our soul have certain desires with which we come into this physical realm, and, once acted upon, these desires have the potential to awaken us to higher levels of consciousness. Before an awakening there may be a feeling that something is missing, something just does not seem right in our life. There is a longing for deeper meaning. Even if you have a great job and a loving family, there may still be something inside pinching at you, telling you there must be something more to all this. You can't put your finger on it, but may question yourself, and question God, if you are religious or believe in some form of higher power. You may wonder, why am I not content with life? Why are things not going my way? Whatever the questions may be, this is the voice of your soul speaking to you. This questioning can last for months, or even years. The soul is searching for a higher consciousness, and this is in fact the first step of an awakening.

What follows is a series of stages that lead to personal transformation. The length of time each stage lasts is different from one person to another, and may last months or years, depending on your own personal growth. You may go back and forth from one stage to another. You may experience many dark nights of the soul, as you wrestle with old patterns or habits that require purging. But don't worry, this is a forgiving process and there is no deadline on it. If the higher self isn't found the first time round, or the cycles of awakening aren't completed, then the experience of an awakening usually repeats itself some years down the line.

The seven stages of a heart awakening

The awakening

Most often this is a beautiful, amazing time, and for a short period it may feel as if you are on cloud nine, with deep blissfulness flowing through you. It's a feeling like no other, and like nothing you have ever experienced before. Love and joy are being transmitted into your body like magic, and the emotions tend to be overwhelming, so much so that you may want to cry. It may feel strange and confusing, and you may not understand what is going on, but you know that something different is happening inside your body. You may have a feeling that your chest is opening up and coming alive, and this feeling is something you never want to end. This is the I AM presence.

The dark night of the soul

Feelings of ecstasy and uplift don't always last, but rest assured that this is quite natural. The dark night of the soul is a major phase in spiritual growth, and few people really escape it. Here, things become very dark, and you are likely to feel lost and scared. Anxiety and depression may creep in, maybe panic attacks. You may feel that you are unable to manage life, and, at its most extreme, that you are facing a void. You may want to isolate yourself, and your eating habits and sleeping patterns may change. The people around you notice that something is up, but somehow they can't reach you. You may worry that this is going to last for ever, but, it is necessary to realise that all these apparently negative feelings serve a purpose. They are there for a reason. The dark night of the soul is there to awaken you, to push you to deeper levels of consciousness. You must first experience a death of the old you, and the dark night of the soul is the death that is followed by a rebirth, to bring forward the new you. This stage is a shock to your system, but it's how you realise that you are the answer to all your questions. You are the one who needs to change, because you can't stay in the pain and sadness for ever.

Exploring healing methods

During this stage you may begin to look for answers, reading and researching, and taking the first steps towards healing yourself. It's here that you become interested in spirituality, mystic arts, magic, numerology and philosophy. You begin to look at your old patterns, belief systems and habits. In time, you probably begin to notice some positive changes taking effect. However, you may still not be cured, and some pain continues to trigger you.

Signs of enlightenment

During this time, you catch glimpses of enlightenment. Your meditation and healing practices will develop. Where meaning was once lost, you will now begin to see and notice how much you have developed. You may look back on your old nature and realise, 'I needed to change myself and must keep going.' This time will likely involve much reflection and increasing understanding of how you once were.

Soul growth

You may start to feel connected to the universe and everything in it. You will now certainly notice how much you have changed, and how much you are growing in all areas of life. Of course, this step will take time, as does any new lifestyle. Now is when you see the spiritual world through a new lens. You will know which practices best work for you, and above all, the meaning that was once not there and that caused much of your soul anguish has now shown up, because you have worked on yourself and your soul has matured.

Surrendering to the journey

So now you have done the shadow work and spent many months if not years improving yourself. But something is still wrong. The pain is still there. Anger and fear may arise, and you may still be hurting. Now comes the time when you have to let go and release the unwanted energy that you're holding onto. This is not always so easy; you may go back and forth a few times and this is normal as the ego always tries to creep back in and take over again. But after some time, you will come to terms with releasing and going with the flow of the universe, allowing your higher self to guide you.

Awareness

Finally, you see the light at the end of the tunnel. The ego is no longer who you are. Some describe this final stage as the death of the ego, although I prefer to say that the ego is still present, but we can decide when to use it. By this last stage you have much more of a feel for who you are, and your personal awareness is continuing to develop; you reach a place of peace and now perhaps realise that you are here to serve others, as well as yourself. The old self is now gone and the new self continues to expand. Our awareness is always growing and our perception changing. I describe this as a staircase effect, and with each step we take up we now experience a mini-awakening.

When will it happen?

You may not know when an awakening is coming, although sometimes it occurs through deep meditation. Generally, though, an awakening is going to happen when we least expect it and when it does it will be in perfect divine timing, when it is most needed. There are, however, a few ways for some individuals to pick up hints as to when an awakening will occur. For example, you are in the questioning stage and you know that something isn't right, but can't put your finger on it. This soul restlessness can be seen as a hint that things are changing, especially if you try and follow it to its core and see what it is really saying. What is your dissatisfaction telling you? What do you most want to do and where have circumstances held you back? Often, our deepest personal desires lead to awakenings, and if you have a strong urge to act on some profound desire, this can be your soul encouraging you. These desires may not always be viewed as morally acceptable by society – for example adultery or illegal drug use – but can often trigger awakenings at some point. This may sound strange but many persons who have for example been addicted to an illegal substance go on to later heal themselves and then support others with their drug addiction.

This is not the case for everyone so it's important to look behind the desire and ask what it is really saying, and explore any restlessness carefully before acting on it. The change you end up with may not always be the one you set out to achieve.

The awakening has physical symptoms which vary from one person to another, and are different at each stage. This can be anything from spots on the skin and rashes to headaches and weepiness. Body and mind are going through so many changes that it is only natural to experience physical changes as well. All our emotions rise to the surface, meaning we may feel joyful and content one minute, but deeply sad and unhappy the next. Sometimes the blissful feeling may last longer, perhaps days or weeks, to be followed by a crash of depression or extreme sadness. This creates a real roller coaster effect. Providing you have no illness or are not worried about a health condition, there is no need to be panicked by this. Rather, try to go with the flow of it. Your body is in the process of an upgrade. Everything in an awakening works in stages, as everything in life is a cycle. Pay attention to the moon cycles and how they may affect your emotions and growth. Writing it down is a good way to document what is happening and to chart your progress and any changes. Pay attention to any patterns and synchronicities. Our spirit guide and healing team like to communicate with us in this way. For example, seeing 999 repeatedly indicates that a certain cycle is finishing and a new one is about to begin.

Kundalini meditation

Disclaimer – be aware of possible adverse effects
Practising this meditation may induce a spiritual awakening. Spiritual awakenings can bring a flood of emotions to the surface so it's important to understand that some of this may be unpleasant or uncomfortable, and can last a few days or a few weeks. It's best if you are in good physical and mental health when you begin this practice. Before proceeding, you may want to speak with a spiritual teacher or healer to guide you through; this is entirely up to you and is only a suggestion if you feel you need support. If in any doubt about your physical or mental health, consult your doctor or other healthcare provider before trying this meditation.

During this meditation you may feel an urge to sway or fall backwards as a result of the kundalini energy rising within you. It is therefore advised that you do this meditation sitting on a bed or sofa.

- First, find a space where you will not be disturbed for at least half an hour.
- Sit up straight, as comfortably as you can.
- Place your feet firmly on the floor to ground them.
- Remember, it's important for you to be relaxed and comfortable.
- Breathe in deeply through your mouth, hold for three seconds, then release your breath out through your mouth, allowing the breath to be exaggerated.
- Repeat this four to five times. Breathing this way helps more oxygen to flow around your body. You may feel a little light-headed or tingly, and that's fine.
- When you feel ready close your eyes, and continue to breathe naturally.
- Now imagine a red-coloured orb or spiral in your pelvic area. See this orb getting brighter and bigger with every inhale.
- After a few moments, or when the orb/spiral is big enough to fill your entire pelvic area, visualise red light moving up just below your navel.
- Now imagine the light is turning into an orange orb/spiral.
- See it growing bigger on every inhale. Allow this orange orb/spiral to fill the area below your navel with its warm orange light.
- When you are ready, visualise orange light moving up your body and into your stomach area. See this light turning yellow.

- Watch in your mind's eye as this yellow light turns into an orb/spiral.
- See it glowing with its bright yellow colour. Let this spiral expand until it fills all of your stomach area.
- When you are ready, see this yellow light moving up into the centre of your chest.
- Once it reaches your chest, allow this yellow light to burst open with loving green light.
- Allow this green light to flow all over your chest area. See it expanding with every breath you take. See the green light spiralling around and filling the space in your chest. Feel its loving energy flowing outwardly.
- When you feel ready, see the green light travel up into your throat area.
- See in your mind as this light turns from green to blue.
- Visualise the blue light turning into a spiral and spinning round in your throat area. Allow the spiral to grow bigger. Watch as the light from the blue spiral travels up and fills your mouth.
- After a couple of minutes see the blue light moving up through you and into the centre of your head.
- Visualise this blue light changing into purple. Allow this purple light to fill your entire head. Imagine it rippling over and into your brain with purple waves of light.
- After a couple of minutes, see the purple light move up and out through the top of your head. As the light travels out of your head, it turns into pure white light.
- Let the light reach about 30cm (roughly a foot) above your head.
- Then visualise this white light shooting back into your head and down through your whole body. Feel as it passes back through each chakra. Feel it going through each spiral, down through your legs and out through the soles of your feet into the ground beneath you.

- When you are ready open your eyes slowly. You may feel tingly or light-headed. Allow yourself a few minutes to sit and take in the experience.

Practise this meditation daily for at least three weeks, and be open to receive the blessings it has to offer.

Chapter 7

Soul connections

The important relationships in our lives, and even the ones that are less important, are not random. Even if they appear to be coincidence, they never are. All the relationships we have are with people from our soul family or soul group. This can be family, friends, lovers, work colleagues, acquaintances – even enemies. All of these people are our soul mates. Soul mates are for support, growth and the evolution of one's consciousness. All soul mates are extraordinarily linked – that is, in a way that transcends the ordinary. Something more binds them together. Some soul connections are more obviously here to support us, for example a parent, grandparent or close friend, while some may not be so obvious, such as a destructive relationship like the bond with an abusive lover. But, all these connections support our spiritual evolution, and are very important relationships, every encounter you experience with them presents an opportunity to delve deeper into the hidden depths of the self.

As human beings having an earth experience, we have become very used to the feel-good sensation we get when something that we see as positive happens in our life. We like the feeling it produces and this is very normal and healthy, and shows that our brain is working the way it should to protect us from harm. However, when something negative happens we view the feelings associated with that as unpleasant and something we don't want to experience again. In reality, though, we are here to transcend all these feelings altogether, and to realise that good or bad, positive or negative, it is only a temporary illusion. It's just an experience along our journey, and it's the energy we choose to focus on this experience that makes it either good or bad, pleasant or unpleasant.

Enjoying the feel-good as much as possible and avoiding the unpleasant is for the most part something we all want from life. However, this is what keeps us reincarnating, as we become too attached to the physical, becoming consumed by earthly pleasures. Remember, many if not all the emotions that we experience are our choice, so in any given situation we can choose to see positive or negative – it really is up to us. Knowing this information, we can truly see ourselves and others at the core, where we are the soul – compassionate, loving, expansive and limitlessly connected with all other beings.

Instead, part of the ego mind's job is to have us constantly competing with one another, and perhaps if this wasn't the case we would never better ourselves, but what we are seeking is in fact within us – a feeling of ongoing peace, wholeness and the ability to connect with our brothers and sisters without fear of shame, rejection or abandonment. The ego is connected to the thinking mind, and the thinking mind is a game player. Now more than ever is the time to set aside outdated thinking patterns. When something shows up in our life that we are unhappy with, we must remember that it's really all our perspective. The feeling is produced inside us, and what is happening on the external side is part of the illusion we came here to transcend. Of course, unpleasant feelings will always arise, that's part of life – but it's what we choose to do with these feelings that counts. We can hold on to them for years, blaming ourselves and everyone around us, or we can give ourselves some time to grieve, then let go and see the situation for what it is. Another experience. Move on, knowing that we got what we needed for our highest growth and so did anyone else involved.

So, what is a soul connection?

This is a connection between two people who are linked on a soul level in a significant way, a way that transcends the earth realm. Whatever your relationship may be, you transcend its social titles, such as lovers, siblings or co-workers, because something much more has brought you together. Destiny is at play. In some cases but not all this may be accompanied by a strong feeling that you have known this person before in a past life, and now has come the time for your souls to reunite again on the earthly realm.

Soul mates

As I explained at the start of this chapter, certain people play a significant part in our lives, and seem to be connected to us in a special way.

During your life here on earth there are certain souls that, while in the spirit realm before reincarnating again, you agreed to pair up with, to be close friends or family. Maybe you decided to be lovers, business partners, or to have children together. These soul mate connections often switch roles; for example, someone that was once a lover in this lifetime becomes a sibling in the next. Soul mates can be people you have known your whole life, like a parent, or someone with whom you have a shorter encounter, but who still had a major impact on your life, for example, a doctor that performed life-saving surgery on you. The purpose of a soul mate is to support you in some way or another – emotionally, professionally, physically – so that you can go on and accomplish what your soul planned while here on earth.

Past life soul mates

You often feel a strong pull towards past life soul mates. This is not a feeling you will experience with all lovers, and you can often sense something different early on in the connection. The chemistry between you both is usually very strong. There is a feeling of, 'I know you from somewhere.' This is energy that has built up over the past lives you have shared together. You recognise each other on a soul level. If you feel as though you have experienced this kind of connection, and want more understanding of its significance in your life, you could visit an experienced past life hypnotherapist who may be able to shed some light on the connection using a technique called past life regression to recover memories of past lives, or you may want to have a psychic reading. (Bear in mind this is not foolproof, and can be upsetting for some people if it touches on sensitive matter. Choose your therapist carefully, making sure it is someone you can trust.)

Although you may feel strong feelings towards a past life soul mate, it does not necessarily mean you are to partner up with them. Remember, this is the energy you are feeling between you both. Energy is neither positive nor negative – therefore it's up to you to make the appropriate judgement based on how you get along and how you both treat each other. Does the other person care about your best interests (and vice versa)? How well do each of you care for the other's needs and wants? Past life relationships are sometimes tinged with past life karma, and therefore there may be times when you have to try and bring healing to the situation.

Karma is not necessarily bad. It's really just the universal law of cause and effect, meaning that every single action produces a reaction. Sometimes either you or the other individual left the previous life hurt in some way or with questions, in which case you find that you tend to pick up where you left off. These relationships can be described as having a roller coaster effect and may not last, as unfortunately they can sometimes bring unendurable agony with them. For some, even just being in the presence of a past life soul mate can amplify the energy one or both may be feeling. You may believe that this is your life partner, someone to hold close to you for ever.

As powerful as they may feel, though, as I said above, past life connections are not always meant to last – instead, they are here to help you in some way. For example, if you share a past life connection with a narcissist, they are here to help you transcend any codependency, lack, or heartbreak from your previous life, depending on what you are here to experience. Overall, they have come into your life to support you in becoming a better version of yourself, and to help you connect with your own true self, both the masculine and feminine within. This is the authentic self or the 'I am' presence, being secure in your self-awareness and ideas, and not feeling intimidated by other people's opinions, connecting and trusting in God/source and completely surrendering to your journey.

Twin flames

Before I begin this section, I must state that we all see things from different perspectives and it's this that shapes who we are. There is no wrong or right answer as our experiences are all so unique, and we build our own right answer for us depending on the conditions to which we are exposed. The idea of twin flames has been confused with the notion of falling in love with another person, when in reality, this relationship is about you and your inner self. To be in their presence is to be stripped of certain illusions you have about yourself and this is not always comfortable, but the twin flame relationship triggers love.

A twin flame is indeed a very special kind of soul mate – a mirror soul, or a divine counterpart, someone who reflects your own behaviours and traits back to you, both positive and negative. There is a theory that twin flames are one soul split into two halves in two different bodies, or two mini-souls of the same over-soul that continuously meet in different lifetimes to assist in the growth of the over-soul or one soul (masculine/feminine) in two individual bodies. Twin flames share the same energetic frequency, meaning that they energetically resonate with one another on a mental, emotional, physical and spiritual level. Each time we come to earth to have a human experience, we have certain limitations we want to overcome, feelings or emotions we want to experience, goals we want to achieve, along with more fulfilling relationships with others or with ourselves. A twin flame often supports you in these areas directly or indirectly, providing you with a scenario you came here specifically to experience, and giving you the opportunity to see life from different perspectives, although these patterns may not become evident until weeks or months into the relationship.

It is not only twin flames who support us in this kind of way – other soul mate connections also help us access our shadow, and these relationships may involve a spiritual bond. It is believed that twin flame relationships are rare, as both individuals need to obtain a certain level of spiritual mastery before they meet. These souls are here to assist in raising the vibration of the world. They may have a similar mission, although it is not always together. As I said above, romantic as the concept may seem, the notion that you will be together is a misconception – indeed, often, it's quite the opposite and these relationships can be platonic. The role and relationship vary among twin flames, but for these divine counterparts the soul connection remains the same.

All of the connections described above are relationship/karma based contracts, involving a shared soul agreement (something which we will look at more closely in the next chapter). There is no need to go searching for any divine counterparts as they will find you when the time is right, often through some unavoidable situation such as working together. Both individuals involved have something to offer the other from the shared experience they go through, like healing growth and love. Spiritual growth comes when you reach a place of being connected to all, a place of no longer feeling in separation but rather a sense of union with yourself and everyone, including all of nature. The evolution we experience needs to be continually nurtured. We are all a divine part of creation and we are all whole enough to feel satisfaction, love and happiness within our own self, without looking for external comforts or people to fill any void. This is a lifelong commitment, and is something that all individuals must continue to work on during the full course of each lifespan.

True love is not to be confused with feelings like attachment, domination, addiction or the fear of being alone. These types of feelings are dangerous and damaging, they can destroy the true energy of love. Compassionate Love is a detached feeling. Gratitude and Compassion paired with detachment equals unconditional love. Now is a wonderful time here on Planet Earth, when many people are healing their karmic ties and understanding their own great truth. As a collective, the planet's vibration is raising. Doing some form of spiritual practice that best suits you such as meditation or yoga can help you access your shadow side and speed up your development, moving you forward in the right direction for you. Allowing time to pass, you will gain the answers to your own unique journey and the soul connections you have.

A companion to share life with is one of the most beautiful features in human experience, but you do not need someone else to make you feel whole. If you are searching for love to fill an emotional gap, then the sad truth is that you will continue to experience conditional love-based relationships. Where you project any kind of incompleteness about the self the universe will send you back relationships that reflect this. The love you are searching for comes from within – true love has no connection with any one person. It's you and always has been you.

Many of us may know this, but continue to face this challenge along our path to higher personal development because we often become attached to the feel-good experience of falling in love. In addition, self-love is an ongoing commitment, and this can be very difficult. When a relationship ends, many of us seek out another. We look to some kind of outside comfort to fill the void, sometimes becoming addicted to some behaviour or substance. These can range from alcohol, drugs, sex, nicotine, our appearance, food, exercise, shopping, validation from others, computer games, caffeine, our job, money, even a certain soul connection. If we become reliant on such things, we risk falling into a trap of unhealthy patterns.

Of course, we need some material comforts, leisure and society to sustain and enjoy life. I am in no way suggesting not to enjoy a few glasses of wine over the weekend with family or friends. However, it's important not to overindulge while still continuing to enjoy life's pleasures, all of which support our mental health and well-being. The key word to remember here is balance. One way to achieve this is by listening to the feelings your body is sending you in any given situation. This is how our intuition speaks to us and it always has our best interests at heart, although this inner skill is often ignored, as we live in a world primarily based on logic.

Do not wait on a divine counterpart or anybody else – enjoy your life and be open to new possibilities. Remember, it's important for you to continue your own healing and to remain conscious of your own patterns. The spiritual community pays quite a bit of attention to the twin flame union, but I believe this often keeps many individuals trapped in a loop. If you really think about it, we would not entertain the concept of a twin flame if we were truly healed, because we wouldn't need it. During the course of an awakening – most likely after an individual has spent months if not years of their life chasing love – there will be a new level of awareness that such chasing (or being chased) is not healthy and merely creates codependency. This is really what our journey is about – freeing ourselves from negative patterns. Remember, a divine connection is an accession tool, that is, a tool to help you rise to your highest potential. Yes, you may share a mission with any given important soul connection in your life, but this will all show up in perfect divine timing if it is a part of your soul's blueprint.

My soul mate is a narcissist

My advice is to continue to raise your vibration and to work on yourself. If a narcissist is a part of your journey, they are likely to be an important soul mate, because these types of relationships push you to look at yourself. If you are not in a high vibrational place, then this kind of relationship has the capacity to challenge you severely at first, so much so that you may feel you are being destroyed, but keep in mind that this is to assist you with your growth. There is a chance that you may have spent previous lifetimes with the narcissist, and that your relationships usually focus around some kind of theme such as abuse, abandonment or betrayal. The narcissist may well be the starting point that triggers 'love', but this is often a fraught and not necessarily stable relationship, and much of this depends on your own unique situation. They may act as your greatest source of inspiration in the present, but in reality, the true twin flame is yourself, and your heart is a perfect balance of masculine and feminine energy.

As stated, energy is neither good nor bad – it's how you react to this energy. Narcissist and empath are names describing an individual's current pattern of relationships and their approach to life. Both these types are sensitive to their surroundings and to other people's energy. All humans have within them positive and negative traits; no one is 100% good and no one is 100% bad – we all have a shadow side and it is needed, often sparking us with inspiration and gratitude for what we have in life. Narcissists like empaths are often very pleasant and likeable, and may involve themselves with helping others, professionally or voluntarily.

Some people may say this is part of the narcissist's false agenda, but really this is who they are. We as humans tend to blame the person for our feelings towards them, when in reality what we are feeling is coming from within us, and is something we need to take care of, not someone else. If we become reliant on someone else for emotional security, or things fall apart, we tend to blame the other person because we have convinced ourselves that we have the right mixture for a perfect love recipe. We must take responsibility for our actions. Calling the narcissist evil, saying negative things about them, or spreading hatred shows that we are no better than they are and, moreover, that they still have our energy, because we are unable to let go of the feelings we believe they have triggered inside of us.

A narcissist is sometimes described as an energy vampire, but no one has the power to access your energy unless you give it to them. We all have the ability to take other people's energy for a brief moment, and at some point we all have done this. We may do this without even knowing it. By simply offering another advice when they are feeling down or upset, we gain energy if we feel our efforts have been appreciated – it gives us a sense of feeling important and valuable. So, in this moment, we have absorbed the energy of another person, because it makes us feel good knowing that we have helped. In fact, it's wise to see a narcissist as someone who has great healing powers, because they show you your worth, even if this is involuntary. Their darkness – or how we have chosen to absorb their darkness – often pushes us towards the light, revealing to us our own traits that need amending or healing.

The narcissist is a soul mate if you are a vibrational match at the time of meeting, and you shared a close bond with them. A vibrational match simply means your soul frequency matches up to theirs, something you may not even realise until you really reflect on your own behaviour and thought patterns. Anyone who has a relationship with a narcissist is a vibrational match for them because this is how energy works. It is not the case that sometimes this was just an unfortunate situation – it's a response to a vibrational condition you have going on inside yourself. No one is ever wrongly placed. If you are having repeated relationships with a narcissist, this is no coincidence. It means there are still lessons to be learned – perhaps a lack of boundaries, maybe giving your power away too easily, or not giving yourself enough time to get to know the other person before entering into a relationship.

It is our intentions that attract certain people into our lives. These intentions can be either conscious or unconscious, and may be for several reasons, but primarily concern what is going to benefit our soul. Only when you raise your own vibration and reflect on your own behaviour or mindset, will you be able to spot the signs and understand why you may be attracting certain situations or people. Raising your vibration does not mean you will never encounter a manipulative person again – it means you will spot the red flags much faster and be able to walk away, with the awareness that there is no need to put your energy into that experience again. Energy is always changing, so our vibration is always changing – everything is a choice and every choice we make reflects the energy we are giving out and receiving back. Changes happen quicker for some people than for others, and when I say change, I mean that we can make a choice. Every day we are faced with a number of choices and it's up to us to use the information and knowledge we have in that moment to make a decision. We can choose to express good rather than bad, positive instead of negative; it really is up to us. If you choose to attune yourself to universal law and the flow of the universe, it responds back to you. In saying that, nature always responds to love and kindness, and once you allow yourself to welcome in love by first taking care of yourself, you then will receive it from the whole world, and create a life filled with happiness.

So is a narcissist a divine counterpart?
Everyone has their own perspective and way of seeing things and everyone's path is unique to them. No one can say that

someone is a soul mate, twin flame or past life connection – it is up to you to make that decision. A professional past life reading may help you reach this decision, but remember, you also have freedom when it comes to sifting psychic advice, and ultimately it is up to you how much of this too you take on board. I personally would say that any of these connections can be a divine soul mate connection. However, it is important for you to judge this with logic as well as with intuition, and to know when it is appropriate to let go of anyone who is not serving your highest growth. Letting go may be the hardest thing to do for that particular contract but the repercussions of staying in an unhealthy relationship often involve lasting damage.

If the relationship with any individual is a divine encounter, you may have both caused each other pain and pleasure during the relationship, as these kinds of bonds are what create a spiritual tie. The pain you caused may have been done knowingly or unknowingly, but the key point is that both of you experience growth as a result of the connection. If you are unsure about any connection in your life, questions to ask yourself may include:

- Do their words match their actions?
- Are they continually hurting you?
- Are you hurting them?
- Is the connection depleting your energy?
- Do you feel good when you are around them?
- Are you experiencing energy shifts as you move through the cycles that encourage you to let go or to continue with them?
- Are you both honest with one another?

These are all clues as to the type of connection you are experiencing. Other people's opinions and labels can create confusion, so instead listen to your inner voice. Think about what this person in your life has taught you, and what you have taught them, not necessarily with words but with actions. Above all, are you both supporting one another's growth by continuing to stay in the relationship?

Hard to let go

I do not recommend spending years and years of your life obsessing over one person because this is not healthy for you. We obsess because we are still trying to control the outcome and make sense of it all. Don't resist the thoughts that may intrude upon you. Instead, allow them to come and then to pass you by. Spend time working on yourself. This obsession, however, remains present as a way of reminding you to connect with the I AM presence within. It's your soul's way of saying there is still work to be done. When the time *is* right for you and you have gone through the cycles, you begin to surrender, learning to go with the flow and the answers you seek come.

Surrendering is an ongoing process. It is believing and trusting in God, the universe, or your higher self, that all that you need and want comes to you in perfect divine timing. From a soul perspective the soul of any divine counterpart loves you very much and is giving you this experience spiritually to grow. Their love for you is eternal. What happens in the 3D – that is, in the here and now – is all a performance like that of a play, and how they behave is not necessarily a reflection of how they truly feel. You can speed up your progress by undertaking some kind of spiritual practice. Stepping away from any connection you are unsure about often gives you time to reflect and get a feel of what is happening. Remember, don't be taken in by appearances – all is not as it seems. Usually, love for someone else acts as a starting point for our journey to ascension and is not necessarily a stable fixture for us, although it may be our greatest inspiration when we set out.

Are you divinely connected to a narcissist?

Below I have listed some ways to help you understand if you are experiencing a divine connection with a narcissist. It's important to bear in mind that in this lifetime your relationships carry karmic energy that needs to be worked through, and any close soul mate connection has the potential to awaken us. Take what resonates from the list and leave what doesn't. You may find that all of these fit your experience, or just one or two. We all have unique experiences and are at different stages of our journey; it would be impossible to list all possibilities. For this reason I have also chosen not to put anyone's journey into a set category, such as twin flames or karmic partners. These are all soul mates and any of these can assist you in accessing your shadow so that you can then begin healing, improving yourself and being of greater service to the rest of humanity. Your soul mission is not so much something you do, but is the energy or passion that drives everything you do, and it starts with how you view your own world.

The most important point from the list is the last one. Many individuals who have experienced an abusive relationship then go on to be a relationship therapist, teacher, counsellor, life coach or some kind of healer. They are often not aware that their abusive journey was all part of their own divine plan, because with the life experience they can now align with their mission.

- You feel a strong connection to this person quite early on in the relationship, as if you have known them in a past life. The pull towards them may be extremely strong.
- You experience an awakening soon after meeting them, or at the end of a relationship.
- The awakening is powerful and has the symptoms of a kundalini awakening – feelings of love, joy and total bliss stemming from your heart centre (see Chapter 6, Spiritual awakening).

- You become deeply interested in spirituality, self-mastery and a relationship with God, spirit or the universe. You now want to make improvements in all areas of your life.
- You become inspired to connect with the unknown realm around you.
- You get to know your self-worth and value as a result of this connection.
- Deep down you know or feel that something is off but at the same time special with this connection.
- You see your own patterns of behaviour; the other person acts as a mirror, and as a result, you want to work on yourself.
- The other person's darkness brings you closer to the light.
- There is telepathy between you.
- Synchronicities begin to play a part in your journey.
- You have not experienced another soul connection like this one.
- You realise how much you love them because you see the bigger picture of how they have helped you to heal, and helped you along your ascension process or development path. This is the biggest sign of a narcissist being an important soul connection – they have helped you to evolve your consciousness. Their actions have pushed you to look at yourself, helping you access your life purpose. The result is an even deeper understanding of life, and a new balance, aligning who you truly are with self-illumination.

Narcissist and empath are both words that have been created to describe two spiritual beings. So can a narcissist be an important soul connection? My answer is yes, because we are all love on a soul level, working together and assisting each other's growth. These divine connections usually involve one of two opposites; although you may share similarities, these are often two very different personalities coming together, like yin and yang, or light and dark, and they act as catalysts for our personal growth. They may be our biggest teacher, healer and source of guidance; at times this pairing is matched as both individuals carry aspects or traits that the other needs in order to evolve. For example the empath learns boundaries from the narcissist.

On the surface this may appear to be a mismatch, but in actuality they complement one another. However, it often takes years or lifetimes for this pair to put aside their differences. They will both fight the connection, but the pull of the bond and the power of love eventually outweigh the fear. Divine connections also can be seen in many movies and doesn't always have to be a romantic partnership. Remember, we have many lifetimes with certain souls with a different scenario playing out each time. In the *Harry Potter* movies, Harry Potter and Voldemort have a spiritual connection. They both need each other to understand their power and are connected on a deeper level, sharing a telepathic bond. Their duel is really a marriage of opposites, so that while they are enemies, they are both supporting each other's growth and sense of purpose, and their lives are intertwined. Close soul mates support each other to grow. They go through a process in which they spiritually transform. This is called alchemy, and is the unity of opposites coming together, even if it's only for a chapter in each other's lives. The goal of spiritual alchemy is to transform not from dark to light but a third energy, spiritual gold energy. This energy brings about unity in the presence of both light and dark. The third energy Transends light and dark and is present in Christ consciousness. Some people may tell you that you have created an unhealthy soul tie, but no soul tie is unhealthy because it serves a purpose in your life. There is a reason for it – for you to grow, heal and develop more compassionate love for yourself and for others.

Synchronicities

Many people view synchronicities and coincidences as signs from the universe, with a particular meaning that relates to our experience, however, they don't seem to us to abide by the laws of cause and effect. They are the strange experiences we often choose to brush off, because they are beyond what we can comprehend. Seeing synchronicities along your journey points to alignment and shows that you are on the right path. They often tie in with angel numbers. For example, the first day I encountered my narcissist was on 11/11/2018. In numerology this can be converted to 11.11.11 (111 being the so-called angel number, associated with new life journeys under the guidance of our angels). 11/11 may also act as a marker or an alert to events that you have placed along your journey. A wake-up call. At the time of meeting my narcissist I didn't know anything about divine connections or numerology. I was definitely dominated by my ego and had my own selfish agenda; I was not even fully aware of how my actions were just as harmful to myself as to others. Although my journey was activated at this point, my awakening started in 2020. Throughout my journey I saw 11/11 each time before my narcissist contacted me, as well other synchronicities related to him. Often these brief encounters with him would be followed by an energetic shift within my psyche. Over time the numbers changed and I began to see different synchronicities related to my path. It was then that it became clear that this connection was about me, and that I needed to know what unhealthy patterns existed both in myself and in others to then see what healthy patterns should be. This is the duality that the divine path offers.

Mantra meditation

Here is where you can create your own mantra meditation for personalised healing to experience more of your true self. This meditation technique is one I hold close to my heart. I personally find manta meditation very healing, and it has helped me a great deal along my own journey. In the case of unhealthy thought patterns or obsessions, it can help change that negative story into a positive one. If you repeat mantras or incantations several times a day, either out loud or in your mind, they will eventually become a part of your subconscious mind. Mantras reprogramme the brain but work even more effectively if done in meditation. I also find that this practice is very good for bringing your energy back to you.

So, to create your own mantra meditation, it's important to know what you want to get out of it, because as part of this exercise you have to come up with your own mantra. This can be two to three sentences long. At the end, thank God, the universe or your higher self.

An example of a mantra can be:

- My positive thoughts guide me to new heights. I am conquering my fears and becoming stronger each day. I thank God and I trust in divine timing and that everything is working out for my highest good.

Repeat your mantra before you begin the meditation. Take about ten minutes for this part of the practice, and then continue saying your mantra at intervals throughout the rest of your day, as and when you have an opportunity.

You may wish to put on some relaxing music.

- Start with focusing on the breath, the most important thing we need is air. All humans depend on it; air sustains life.
- So, focus on the air.
- The air we take in and the air we let out.
- Focus on the breath.
- With each breath, pause for a count of two.

- Say to yourself, 'Breathing in on the inhale.'
- Pause for a count of two.
- And then say to yourself, 'Breathing out on the exhale.'
- Continue to repeat this until you feel relaxed.
- Now begin to repeat your created mantra in your mind.
- Pause for a count of two each time before you begin it.
- Notice the emotions that come up inside. Don't engage with them, but put a name on what you are feeling, then let it pass.
- Repeat for ten minutes.

Then continue to repeat as many or as few times as you like throughout your day.

Chapter 8

The soul contract with a narcissist

What is the soul contract? Many people believe that life is a strange mystery and that the people we meet are random connections that happen to pop into our lives, when really there is a spiritual map that you, your soul, created. If you can imagine, the soul wants to create and experience itself in all manners of forms during each lifetime, and specific timelines and experiences are linked in with this plan, so that you are able to achieve all you (or your soul) wants. This plan also has details of any important soul contracts, with both souls having a certain agreement to carry out a certain action or task. This includes the dates when you encounter such contracts, which can be viewed as divine timing and are something to which you should pay close attention.

Our soul plan involves karma, unresolved issues from past lives that we all carry, and the soul puts us in situations that expose us to this unresolved karma so that it can be brought up again for healing. Our parents, legal guardians and other family members are usually the first exposure we have to our unhealed karma, however, it is most usually lovers, a spouse, siblings or close friends that have the most influence on our spiritual and personal growth, and it is often within these connections our unresolved karma shows up. With that being said we all have our own talents or gifts that will then support us throughout our life journey, and with the healing that needs to take place.

When we physically die, we begin our journey home back to the spiritual realm where we are greeted by our guides and other members of our soul group, loved ones like our friends, family and other close relationships. Some of these souls have the same level of awareness as we do, and they form part of our support group. Further learning and healing take place in the spirit realm. Before we begin a new incarnation on earth, our soul then creates what is called a soul plan. In this plan we put together all the contracts between us and other souls we are to encounter here on earth. Some of these are past life connections while others are new. Each and every soul contract that is created has benefits for both souls involved. This ranges from the brief conversations we have with people in the supermarket, whom we may never see again, to the lifelong relationships we create with friends or a spouse. Now, because this is a plan and free will exists, there are different possibilities with regard to people we have planned to encounter. Our soul knows we may choose to go one way or we may choose another but, generally, these encounters or paths are designed to lead us to the same place eventually, a place of bliss, joy, fulfilment, honesty, trust, forgiveness and a greater knowledge of ourselves. Remember the soul always wants what is best for you, however, in any given experience we may not know what that looks like, and a painful experience is often designed to ignite a new path.

Some relationships involve unhealed karma from previous past lives, and these tend to be the relationships that impact us the most. Different contracts serve different purposes – some offer healing, while others are there to clear any past life power imbalances, meaning that a soul who shared a past life with, for example, an abusive father will pop up again as another player in this life. Perhaps now it is the abusive father's turn to experience the abuse they dished out in a different kind of scenario, and this balances the karma. Some contracts are there to be cleared and the energy balanced, while others may have a mixture of both healing and the balancing of energy. There is an infinite amount of possibilities; it all boils down to what you (the soul) is going to benefit from. Your path is uniquely designed for you.

The soul contract with the narcissist

The soul contract you create with a narcissist plays a very important part in your life, and if you have had a romantic relationship with a narcissist this could quite possibly be the most important soul contract for you in this lifetime. You will know if it is from the impact it has had on your life. All souls seek the experience of giving and receiving love, so you may be wondering, 'Why would my soul plan be to be abused?' Well, this contract is unique in the way that it is designed to push you to your higher self. If you are in a relationship with a narcissist, then you and they would have agreed that in this lifetime you would support each other's growth – to see things from another person's perspective, to learn and teach one another (perhaps you need some of their traits and they need some of yours), and to reach higher levels of self-love and compassion for yourself and others. This is all to aid in your spiritual progress and is part of the natural flow of development that humans are prompted to follow during their evolutionary process here on earth. The narcissist is in effect an ascension tool to enable you to connect with your higher self – whether you see them as a divine soul mate or a karmic connection, it is all leading you in the same direction.

If you were in a long-term relationship with a narcissist and have now gone no contact, you may now be realising more about your own self-worth. Even if you are still with them, some part of you may be starting to understand this. This is what the narcissist is for. From a psychological aspect, they are viewed as a person who is in their ego or who only cares about themselves; from a spiritual aspect these are people who are often dominated by their shadow side, and who may influence a partner or spouse to fall into a trap of negative patterns, but if this is the case then both individuals need to work on raising their vibration. However, these cycles can offer an individual a chance to free themselves from the narcissist's chains, or the soul binding you both share. If you have ended up in a relationship with one, they are there indirectly to push you to know your own self-worth, and to grow love and compassion.

It's likely that you may have childhood wounds that centre around similar patterns of behaviour. Being with a narcissist is designed to trigger these wounds so that they can resurface and you can work on healing yourself. As healing is a big part of our unique mission, this can take years and cycles will often repeat, so don't be so hard on yourself if this happens – it only means that you are to gain something more from the cycle. Remember, a broken leg is a physical wound that takes some time to heal, and it's the same with emotional wounds. In fact, they may take even longer to heal, but once they do, you will be a much stronger person and your soul will be more evolved. This is when you can go on and help others to heal. Being of service to others is how we fulfil our life mission and our soul's desires, and this can be done in many ways. For example, once you have had a relationship with a narcissist and have reached a place where you feel more balanced (remember self-care is an ongoing process), you may wish to go on and help others who have experienced the same kind of abuse.

Many of us have unknowingly received faulty programming, either from society, our family or just in general. We have been programmed to believe that when abuse happens to us, we are the victim. When really no one is a victim. Victim mentality keeps us on a low vibration and suggests that the narcissist is to blame, but, no one is to blame. To agree to be a victim is to imply that your soul didn't plan all of these experiences for your highest growth. Now, you don't need to believe in soul contracts, but it does help you experience life with greater ease because you know you are the creator of your life. Understanding why this has happened to you, and knowing that you put all of this in place, will support you in raising your vibration and aids with the healing process.

Knowing this, you can take responsibility for your own self. Being able to do this comes from a place of true understanding, wisdom and courage; blame gives your power to others and thus leaves your healing in their hands. In this knowing you can forgive yourself and let go. This is the key to healing – letting go of the hurt and the pain. This can be done so much more easily when you start to see that you are not a victim, you can't be and never have been a victim of life's circumstances. You may feel stuck at times, but this is connected to the same illusion of victimhood and can be broken at any time.

You are a powerful, wise, loving soul that has lived many lifetimes. You will not experience the same situation again if you do healing work, because when you make the changes needed to release the karma, this new evolved energy is imprinted in your soul memory. For example, if there is a pattern of abuse throughout many lifetimes and you transcend it in this lifetime, it is recorded in your soul memory and reflects in your evolution.

Many people will tell you that if you felt love for the narcissist then it wasn't real and you are just one of their victims. This again is not true. What you felt is the I am presence. On a soul level, love is always present and always there. The narcissist does love you on a soul level, but their personality is in darkness and may not be able to feel such emotions, or is too afraid of them. So, they feel more comfortable not letting the light in. Once you realise and accept this truth, you can also heal more quickly. It's not about holding on to the person, trying to make them change – instead it's about being able to forgive, accept and let go, so that you can heal and move forward. It's about clearing the karma between you, learning the soul lessons and moving on – but with love instead of regret, guilt or wanting to take revenge.

The narcissist is designed to change you on many levels, and the real changes can only take place once you step away from them. The transition is likely to take a few years, but you will be a better version of yourself afterwards, and in a much better place. During the transition, you may begin to question every aspect of yourself and to start noticing your own patterns. This can take the form of negative thinking about yourself or others, along with other unhelpful habits such as being too open, too giving, or too forgiving, or not able to speak your truths.

Our thought patterns can endure for years, and because we are so wired with these thoughts we don't even realise we have them – they have become subconsciously ingrained. Many of these thoughts tend to be judgemental, or to involve negative ways of thinking. If we become obsessive about a person we are more likely to eventually notice and become more conscious of our thoughts. The narcissist indirectly shows us we need to change the story. The story in your head gradually changes from a negative to a positive one. First, this involves replacing the obsessive thoughts about them with something else – a big step in itself and can take some time. Secondly comes the opportunity to go deeper into your own mind, and to begin to change all your patterns of thinking. Realise that when you are connected to the story of a situation, like negative thoughts towards the narcissist, you are giving your power to the situation, which can lead to more negative emotions. A simple technique to use to help with this is catching yourself in the act when old memories of the narcissist arise. Each time this happens replace these thoughts or memories with a different memory, either something positive you really enjoyed, or it can be made up – for example visualise yourself somewhere pleasant. Like on the beach or in a flowery meadow. The key to doing this is to stick to the same memory or visualisation each time so it becomes embedded in your subconscious.

Let go
Let it go, and don't be too hard on yourself. Letting go doesn't have a time limit, and can take months or even years. It all

depends on your contract with the person. Perhaps you have learned all you can from them, and they have learned from you, although this does not limit the love from your heart. To speed up your healing, step away from the narcissist, reflect and meditate. Ask your spirit guides for support, and to show you the best healing routes for you in a way you are going to understand. It's highly probable that the contract with a narcissist will lead you on to a more fulfilled life. Nothing is more valuable than your experience. This outweighs any qualification, because you have lived through it and healed, whether you did this with the support of professionals or used self-healing methods. All of us who have experienced this kind of behaviour have a different story to share. You have your own unique journey that can inspire others. This is the true beauty of the relationship; how can you not love the person who has given you all the tools to be a better person and then to go and support others in one way or another.

Never believe you can't do something because you can – it may take time and effort on your part but you can do anything you put your mind to. Taking the first step is always the hardest part, but once you really get stuck in, you will probably wonder, 'What took me so long to do this?'

Feelings of anger, resentment, blame, wanting to take revenge, or feeling you have something to prove, mean you are still unhealed and you have not reclaimed your energy. Call your energy back and send back love and compassion. Some people carry negative feelings toward the narcissist for years, but remember this process is about you. The journey is about self. Speed up your growth by letting it go and seeing how much you have gained from having them in your life. By doing this you are helping them raise their vibration and that of the whole planet.

Many people who have experienced abuse blame their abuser and, while this is entirely natural, it often means they take many years to heal and to forgive that individual. If you understand the law of cause and effect and the nature of the karmic cycle (which often stems from past lives), it is not anyone's fault – it is purely for growth purposes, and so that you can then go on and spread more light in the world. Your soul agreed to this during this lifetime, and to all the experiences that come with it. It is only a temporary phase in the eternal life of your soul. Pain does not last for ever in any situation. You may think, 'Then does that mean I have to suffer in order to grow?' The answer is no, you don't have to suffer at all, if you choose to raise your vibration and get into alignment with who you truly are. This then creates more positive energy, and new experiences will come into your life, as you are now working with the universal law of cause and effect to create positive karma.

The narcissist is part of your soul cluster and if there are still negative feelings between you when you pass away, the chances are that you are coming back to this realm with a similar scenario to try again to offer peace and heal the situation. You may decide to switch roles in the next life, and this is to understand how each other felt and to balance the karma. Everyone who has experienced some kind of abuse is probably dealing with karma. If they have lived through it, then it's because it's part of the blueprint. Once karma has been worked through, there may be a new life with different priorities. Some people end up working in some kind of healing field, or a job where they can be of service and help others, such as a teacher, healer, parent, humanitarian, counsellor or therapist.

One way to help you recognise your own patterns and break karmic patterns is to begin journaling and documenting your dreams. Keep a separate diary for both. Listen to your feelings especially if you feel a sudden spark or change in emotion; this is often a sign you need to focus upon and is one way the universe will communicate with you. Try to jot down any feelings. This doesn't have to be pages and pages – it can simply be a few lines in your journal about your feelings, the time, date, place you were, or whatever feels relevant to you. The same applies to a dream journal. Keep it by your bed and write in it as soon as you wake up. Take a few moments and ask yourself how the dream made you feel – this will help give you an interpretation. Remember the universe and your healing team of spirit guides and angels exist to guide you and activate your mind, but it is still up to you to make a decision.

As always, meditation can help you explore your inner processes and, sometimes, when the work of karma becomes demanding, you may need comfort. The following meditation, Loving the inner child, will help soothe and strengthen you as you wrestle with karmic patterns.

Loving the inner child meditation

- Find a comfortable space and lie down, making sure you will not be disturbed for 20 minutes.
- Take a few deep breaths to relax and calm your mind.
- Now think of a time when you were a child, a time when you were sad, upset or felt let down in some way. Picture the memory in your mind.
- Take a few more deep breaths and close your eyes.
- Now imagine yourself as you are now, in this present moment.
- See yourself as you are now entering into that childhood memory or timeline.
- Go over to the child you used to be, and tell them who you are.
- Explain that you are them from the future – their future self – and that everything is going to work out just fine.
- Give them a hug and smile at them, and tell them how much you love them.

- Allow them to talk with you, and reassure them that if they ever need you, you are always there.
- Spend as much time as you like with the child you once were.
- When you feel ready, say goodbye. Give them another hug.
- Imagine a portal of light opening up for you to step into.
- Walk through this light that leads you back to the present moment.
- Take a few more deep breaths.
- And when you are ready open your eyes.

Use this meditation whenever you feel called to, when your inner child needs you, or when you experience a painful memory from the past. Look at it as your inner child calling for you to support them.

Chapter 9

The spiritual connection with a narcissist

Different types of spiritual connections are often formed with the people closest to us, including our many soul mates. It's important to love and honour all the relationships in our life, as they are there to support us when faced with the bigger or more difficult soul connections, while we do the same for our loved ones, so that we are all working together as a continuous network for one another.

If you share a spiritual connection with a narcissist, you are connected on a deeper level. At first you may have felt intensely drawn to this person for reasons you can't even explain. Often this is because that individual has something much more to offer, and the experience they provide gives you the chance to know yourself better. The magnetic pull towards them may be due to the past lives you have shared together, so that the energetic bond is stronger than usual soul mate connections. Often this person changes you in a profound way – life is not the same after meeting them.

Spiritual connections don't have to be limited to a romantic partner. We can have these bonds with close friends or family members, but, this said, it is often with romantic connections that we tend to experience such a link. The connection is deeper than just attraction – it has the power to hit you mind, body and soul. These types of bonds are formed with the people who trigger many different emotions within us and we may also trigger them, with both positive and negative emotions.

The connection is not limited to the three lower planes of existence, that is, the physical, emotional and mental levels. It goes beyond the illusion or the 3D world we live in now, and extends above this. This connection is on a spiritual level;

however, often these connections operate in the lower spiritual plane. You may find that you share a telepathic bond with the person, have very vivid dreams of them, or even share the same dreams or begin to experience synchronicities around them or when they come into your life.

The connection with a narcissist often opens you up to the spiritual world. You were once asleep, and now you are awake. This type of relationship defies normal psychological explanations. It can feel demonic or dark, or you may even wonder if you are losing your sanity. Uncomfortable as these feelings undoubtedly are, they are there for a purpose – to make you aware that your own vibration needs raising. Some people say that the narcissist takes your soul. Yes, it may feel that way, but understand that no one can take your soul. It is not something that can be taken, it is the essence of you, your intellect, emotions, will, it is your consciousness. Your soul is immortal, the higher part of you that is always connected to source. What is happening here is some kind of spiritual binding. If the connection is past life related, or even if not, the aura often becomes damaged so that the wound can become apparent. A person may have unhealthy patterns or ways of thinking but it may not be so obvious until the wound shows itself. This can be unpleasant or uncomfortable but it's needed so that these feelings can be felt. These feelings are encouraging a shift in your consciousness prompting the individual to take action in repairing mind, body and spirit. So, when the entanglement is formed or it resurfaces again in this life, your auric field becomes damaged. The aura is a field of energy that completely surrounds the physical body. It is made up of several layers and it can expand or contract depending on a number of different factors such as how healthy you are or how emotionally or psychologically you feel at any given moment. Like the chakras the aura is a channel of energy and can get clogged due to illness or stress. The aura has several different layers, and the deeper any unhealthy behaviour penetrates these layers, the more likely you are to feel physically and mentally drained, to the point where it can feel as if heavy forces are anchoring you down.

In this case, you do have the power to call your energy back to you and heal yourself, as I described earlier in this book (see the meditation on pulling your energy back to yourself at the end of Chapter 5). It may take a bit of time and you may feel you want the help of a spiritual healer as well – for example Reiki practitioners specialise in chakra and aura cleansing. They help to channel universal life energy, which is a natural expression of life's infinite intelligence. Reiki is a method of self-healing as we all have this energy freely available to us, but a practitioner can provide a bit more support and guidance. If you decide to address the issue independently you can ask your spirit guides or higher self for restitution. This is a way of calling your energy back to you, and can be done by using prayer or a mantra and repeating it as often as you like, or when you feel your energy is being tugged at any place, any time. A simple mantra to use may be, 'Any of my energy that is with (their name), I ask that it return to me, I wish no harm to come to anyone. Any of (their name) energy I have with me I ask that it returns back to them. I wish no harm to come to anyone.' Repeat this several times out loud.

If you have felt such a profound, deep connection with someone, this is a blessing and is in your destiny, although it may not currently feel this way. Understand that this connection has been created to accelerate your spiritual journey, and opens your eyes to a whole new world, with a cycle of destruction and then rebirth. This may sound harsh but this is the fastest path towards growth. The cord of attachment you have with the person can be used to benefit you both. Draw on it to send this individual healing love, which is also helpful for yourself as it helps balance the karmic wounds. Once you are out of the obsession stage, you enter a new stage of your awakening, the stage of self-realisation – that you are your greatest love and always have been. Then, it is up to you to decide if and how you want to let go. Letting go of a connection with a narcissist and stepping away gives you a chance to see things from a bigger perspective and to access your own feelings more deeply.

I would advise you to give yourself the time you need to heal before moving on to a new relationship. If you suspect that this may be a past life lover, it's important not to have too many energy streams running out into past life events at the same time as this can drain your life force energy and lead to more of the same experiences playing out in your life. For example, having repeated negative thoughts about the narcissist, or continuing to choose old beliefs keeps you stuck in the same vibrational spectrum. This has the power to call in more of the same experiences.

If you can't stop thinking about them, continue to do healing work. However, this can be a sign that another cycle with them is approaching and further learning is to take place. Remember, this was all divinely orchestrated to help you form better habits of thought and a deeper knowledge of yourself that should now stay with you for the rest of your life, providing you now choose to continue on the path of self-development. The obsessive thinking won't last for ever but it has to be worked through, layer by layer. As we are all unique, it all depends on how you experience the different cycles; be gentle with yourself while it plays out. Let the thoughts come and let them go; try to focus your attention elsewhere. When the obsessive thinking stops, you know you have reached a great milestone in your evolution.

Now, you may wish to break this connection or telepathic bond. However, this tie has been created for deeper wounds to be healed, wounds that often stem from childhood or past lives. The bond is there so that you can experience it and it can be used to your advantage, perhaps by strengthening your intuition, or by working through karma. You are able to bring your own talents and gifts to this process. We all have our own unique soul frequency and this is made up of multiple layers of frequency streams that are a combination of things, such as inherited family beliefs, cultural and societal beliefs, personal beliefs and values based on life experiences, and thought forms or concepts you align with or are attuning to. When we experience an abusive relationship, our beliefs and patterns of thinking usually come to the surface slowly, so that they can be thought through, considered and released if necessary. This is part of the awakening process.

Awakening occurs at different times for us all, because we are all different and experience things differently. If your awakenings are linked to relationships and you have been with a narcissist, then you will probably experience an awakening after the relationship has ended. However, it can occur much earlier. Either way, this is a gift that your soul planned for you – to go through an awakening and then to heal yourself. It's a very beautiful event. There are no accidents in life. You were probably pushed to your limits and didn't realise you had such profound strength, and this is growth for your soul. Bear in mind it's only because we have become attached to feeling good (or that feel-good feeling that positive experiences bring) that we resist, not realising this is part of the illusion and that this is what keeps us coming back to the earth realm. Most of us allow our outer world to be a reflection of our inner world. When in reality, things are not positive or negative, rather just different tones of your being.

Telepathy within spiritual connections

All of us are connected, and so we all have the ability to connect telepathically. For example, you are thinking about someone, and you receive a call from them at that moment. The narcissistic connection may show more obvious signs of a telepathic link, like having shared dreams, or experiencing very vivid dreams of them. This can be viewed as a form of abduction – that they have hijacked your soul – but this happens if you are in a place of darkness, or have limited boundaries or are unbalanced in some way. All of these experiences are to enlighten you and prompt you to come back to your true self. You may even have dreamt about this person before they came into your life. This is your soul's way of warning you that you are about to have an encounter with a person who is going to make you aware of different interdimensional levels of existence.

Mind control and mental manipulation can be experienced within abusive relationships, whereby one person is able to control the mind of their target by altering their thoughts, perception or memories. Depending on the user's skill or power, this may be done by making continuous suggestions over a long period of time. Some people are able to induce a trance-like state similar to hypnosis in their target, rendering them completely subject to the user's control. Some narcissists are adept at controlling the minds of multiple people simultaneously.

Psychic communication opens a psionic line of communication with another individual. (Psionic relates to the ability to use the mind in telepathic and other psychic activities.) This line is purely for communication and not for mind-reading, as the person can only hear or feel what the target wishes to send back. This form of telepathy can be experienced within a healthy spiritual connection.

Thought manipulation is similar to mind control. In some forms of mind control, the individual is able to control what another person is thinking, to induce them to share or to confess secrets, or even completely shutting down their target's thinking. This can happen in more severe types of abuse.

With emotional manipulation, the user is able to sense and control their target's feelings and mood. In more extreme cases, they may be able to channel a particular emotion and manifest its energy on the physical plane. For example, the target may begin to experience intense sexual feelings, and then hear from the narcissist, who feels the same. This is telepathy sent through senses.

Clairsentience, also known as clear feeling, is very common; indeed, most people have this psychic ability but are unaware of it. You may feel it when the narcissist is about to ring you, is close by, or is going to come and see you.

Psychic torture is another form of manipulation that takes place within spiritual ties. This enables the user to torture their target mentally, spiritually and psychologically, and is linked in to extreme mind control and severe abuse.

Some empaths or sensitive individuals are able to do what is called emotional healing. They are able to access others' wounds and burdens, and help shift their energy to a more positive level. This power may involve therapeutic touch or massage, and offers warmth, consolation, and an ability to see the brighter side of things which can be immensely comforting to those in need. People who have gone through abusive relationships tend to be sensitive to others' distress and to have this talent.

Claircognizance or clear knowing is another psychic gift. This is when you 'just know' something – often something about another person which they haven't told you – or the answers to questions come to you out of the blue. It may involve vivid dreams, flashes of insight or memory, or glimpses of the person in parallel realities or past lives. It may also come as a premonition that acts as a warning from our healing team. Here it's important to follow your intuition. Send the situation love and healing through your heart chakra, and maybe wait before rushing in and getting involved.

The connection with a narcissist may trigger your psychic abilities in general. For example, you feel or sense something different in their touch from the beginning – this is called clairtangency (psychometry), and is another psychic ability which involves receiving information through physically touching an object, person, animal or place. Often the psychic information triggered by the physical touch comes in the form of a strong feeling or sense that this is an important person in your life. If you are experiencing dreams about a particular individual, are they positive or negative? How do they make you feel? This can be a big clue as to what you have experienced with them in past lives, or as a forewarning for what is to come, so don't ignore such dreams. Keep a record of them in your journal.

The telepathy with this person may begin before you meet them, and you may have been shown this person in your dreams beforehand. We are all constantly sending out messages energetically communicating to the universe through our thoughts and emotions, and in turn the universe sends us back experiences that match that vibration on the physical plane. If we have a deep longing for such a connection, it is very likely that it will manifest in some form or another. Now, this doesn't mean that we always get what we think we want. Instead, we get what is best going to serve us, and anyone involved in raising our vibration and the planet's consciousness. For example, Sally has gone through a string of unsuccessful relationships. She can't understand why she is unable to find a perfect match. This is because she is constantly unconsciously communicating with the universe by sending out messages that she wants the right man to be with her, but generally she has negative thoughts towards the men in her life like her father, her brothers and her boss. These thoughts are a reflection of her subconscious feelings, and in turn the universe sends back experiences that will continue to promote her in raising her vibration until Sally learns to change her general attitude towards men.

If you have experienced a relationship with an emotionally abusive person your unconscious mind sent out messages to the universe to bring you the right person for you. This doesn't necessarily mean someone who will love you unreservedly, but someone who will support you in knowing yourself better and in understanding any limited boundaries that the shadow self has imposed. Without this relationship, you may never have known what is healthy, and what red flags look like. At first, you may have felt as if you have met the perfect person for you, only for it all to come crashing down when you realise what is going on. However, this all happens for a reason – to trigger healing – and often starts when you have been emotionally drained for a long while, or you reach a breaking point. This point is different for all of us. Some of us can withstand years of this kind of abuse, others not as long.

The key point, however, is that this connection can bring awareness of your own gifts, abilities, and talents, and you become far more alert to what is going on in your life and the improvements that you need to make. Having our emotions triggered in this way plays a big part in our spiritual maturity, because our emotions often get us closer to knowing our true self. Any spiritual experience can be emotionally powerful. When we experience any type of grief that triggers us, and the storm passes, we appreciate a new level of happiness, spiritual understanding and wisdom. We become aware of how powerful our emotions are, and how they have the ability to make or break us – if we let them. The solution is not allowing ourselves to become too attached to any emotion, as they are fluctuating and will always change. At times we experience joy, and other times sorrow. If we become too attached, we run the risk of being dependent on a pattern, habit or emotional experience to fulfil us.

By using some kind of spiritual practice and asking our healing team/spirit guides to help, we are enabled to stay calm in difficult situations. If any emotions come up that you don't like, it's important to allow them to rise to the surface. This may take some time depending on what we are going through, and it may be uncomfortable, but you don't have to do anything – just sit with the emotions and listen to what they are, and what they are telling you. We all experience emotions differently and we have the ability to become stuck with them, but if we see them for what they are, we become less attached, so giving space for balance to return.

When we incarnate on earth, at that precise moment all information about our soul comes with us. This is the soul's blueprint, and it may be that the narcissist is part of yours. Some people like to investigate this further by sourcing different information from numerology, Tarot cards, or astrology. Understanding or decoding your soul contract in this way is valuable if it offers insight into karma that needs to be rebalanced, and a way of connecting with universal guidance. Once we begin to address these karmic patterns, we are then able to start living our highest truth and happiness. It may be helpful to look at your birth or natal chart and, if you can, the birth charts of the significant people in your life. Synastry is all about relationship astrology and can provide you with clues and incredible insight as to how individuals interact with one another, by understanding the dynamics that are at play when two people come together.

However, what is more important is that you look at your own birth chart and use it as part of your spiritual guidance. Those who have the foresight to investigate their birth chart are those most likely to become masters of their own destiny. All of your chart is important; however, the 12th house, Chiron placement, north node and south node placements give you an indication of past lives, and what you are now here to do, learn, and heal in this lifetime. Many of the experiences of our first 30 years are related to the south node and who we were in our past life. However, as we have now entered the age of Aquarius, the planet's vibration is rising and many people are becoming aware of their karma younger than 30, and awakening to their north node or soul's purpose sooner.

The Akashic records meditation

The Akashic records meditation can help you enter the quantum field, heal past life wounds and access any information you need for your spiritual healing.

The Akashic records are believed to be located on the quantum field and to hold the information of all universal events – all souls, thoughts, words, emotions and deeds that have ever taken place, held on a plane of the eternal now. Anyone can access these records using a number of different methods such as meditation or a pathway prayer. The records are not judgemental and there is no wrong or right way to approach them. Consider carefully how you feel and what best suits you.

The quantum field is a higher vibration that is above the three lower planes of existence (physical, emotional and mental planes). However, all the fields are connected. The energy of the quantum field can be used as a healing tool, as it is at the energy level of pure creation and unconditional love. Once you begin to visit the field regularly and become comfortable in its energy, you can then prepare any questions you may have. The answers could come in a number of different ways like a feeling, a flash of insight, images in your mind, or a dream.

Below I have created a meditation to assist you in accessing the Akashic records. These records are right here – all you need to do is relax, surrender and allow yourself to enter. To start with, it would be a good idea to get a feel of the healing energy in the Akashic records before you ask any questions. You know you have entered the records when you reach a space of nothingness and have completely let go of any expectation.

- Begin by setting an intention to access the Akashic records on the quantum field.
- Find a comfortable space, allowing yourself at least 30 minutes of time to yourself.

- Lie down, and when you are ready, take a few deep breaths.
- Repeat this five or six times, breathing deeply in through your nose, then out through your mouth.
- Allow your body to become completed relaxed.
- Pay attention to any sensations of tingling you may be experiencing, perhaps in your hands or feet.
- Now bring your attention to the space between your eyebrows, where your third eye is located.
- Focus on this area and sense any tingles that you may be feeling in your third eye.
- Pay attention to this area for a few minutes.
- When you are ready, visualise a small purple light on the area you have been focusing on (the third eye).
- See this purple light becoming bigger and bigger until it expands to the size of a tennis ball.
- Hold the light in the centre between your eyes, simply observing its glow for a while.
- Now visualise this purple tennis ball of light becoming absorbed into your brain.
- Notice any sensations you feel as this happens.
- Let go of any sort of outcome and enjoy where you are at in this present moment.
- Spend as much time as you like here, and when you are ready open your eyes.
- Remain lying down for an extra minute or so, just enjoying the feeling of relaxation and contentment, or perhaps picking up on any feelings or emotions that come up.

Practise this meditation as often as you like. Remember, this meditation is designed for you to get a feel of the energy in the Akashic records. As you become more familiar with it you can now go and ask the record any questions you have. You may wish to document in your journal any ideas, thoughts or feelings that you experience after each meditation.

Chapter 10

Holistic healing methods

I wrote this book as a healing tool to help others like myself see that we are all connected and that we should always love the narcissist and forgive the pain that you have both experienced. No one is at fault. Healing comes from love. Growth comes from love. If you can and when the time is right, teach your narcissist love by having boundaries with them. This may involve letting them go and having no contact. It may involve using the grey rock method. But try to hold love in your heart, and let go of negative feelings like guilt, resentment or anger towards them as this may continue the karmic cycle and delay spiritual growth. Have acceptance for who they are.

If you are having repeated relationships with narcissists, and wondering why this is happening and why you are unable to find someone who will love and appreciate you, you must first create a relationship with yourself. Don't rely on anyone to give you that which you can get from yourself. Learn to come into alignment with who you truly are. Love is a beautiful feeling that happens within you. It's a powerful energy. It's not a transaction between two people. Whenever you experience the energy of love, these feelings are created by you and it happens because your emotions become pleasant. Feelings form when the brain assigns a meaning to the emotion you have experienced. Really, you don't need anyone to love you – that's part of the illusion, because the feeling of love is internal.

I have talked about the importance of self-love, however, with relationship trauma, healing comes not only from loving yourself, but from having positive relationships in your life and being able to express gratitude and be yourself. It's not just the love from within that will help us in healing – it is also having other relationships with people we can trust and talk to. This way, we get the chance to see and experience how healthy relationships feel. Remember relationships are never just about you – they are about the ALL. If an individual has positive relationships in their life, they are likely to feel more positive about life in general, and this is because we have a relationship with everything from our family and co-workers to our career.

Below I have listed different healing methods. Some I have discussed earlier in this book. You can try several of these – find what suits you. First and foremost, it is important to embrace all your experiences.

- Aromatherapy has the power to awaken our sense of personal power and to open the solar plexus chakra (the feminine powerhouse). A way to do this is by burning fiery incense and essential oils like saffron, musk, sandalwood, ginger or cinnamon. Always remember to do this safely: never leave incense unattended, and burn away from curtains, furniture or other flammable surfaces.
- Express yourself creatively, perhaps by doing some kind of artwork, writing, knitting or any activity that focuses your attention on the present moment.
- Use your experience of traumatic relationships to do a job you enjoy. It can lead you to a life with greater purpose.

Spend time with loved ones – this can help everyone to build confidence, self-esteem, communication and strength. Our bonds with loved ones have the ability to remodel and rebuild the ability to love ourselves.

- Go on outings to places you like. Spending time in nature can help to reduce the symptoms of anxiety and depression. Studies have shown that time in a green environment can improve your mood and self-esteem.

- Taking up a new hobby offers an unparalleled level of engagement. While reducing stress, it also gives you a chance to socialise and helps you cope with setbacks and challenges in a healthy way.
- Not everyone has someone to talk with or get support from, and in this case you may wish to consult a therapist or other professionals. Even if you do have people you can talk to, getting outside professional support may be a good idea as it is unbiased, and can offer different strategies of coping.
- Play! Being more playful in general helps to soften your mood and live in the present moment. If you have children or get the opportunity to observe them, see how good they are at living in the moment – not worrying about tomorrow or what's happening next week. The same goes for pets – we can learn a lot from having a pet. This companionship can be a great source of comfort and motivation.
- Expressing gratitude helps lift your mood. People who show gratitude for the positive things in life tend to be happier and more optimistic in general.
- Talk with God, and with your healing team of spirit guides and angels. We all have feelings of worry, irritability and anxiety, but when you are experiencing trauma, or have experienced it, these feelings tend to be heightened. Praying is a way of telling God or your higher self how you are feeling and you can bring out any emotions, allowing them to come to the surface. It doesn't matter how desperate you are, and you can be as real and honest as you like. Prayer is one place you don't have to pretend.
- Lean on friends. True intimacy comes from friendship and the conversations we have with one another. Our soul mates or friends are all around us. If you look with open eyes, you will see them – they are our neighbours,

work colleagues or the individuals we meet once a week at book club or in the pub.

- Express yourself through writing in a journal or even writing a letter to anyone who has hurt you or done you wrong. You don't need to post it – this is just a way of expressing how you feel or saying anything that needs to be said. If you like, you can ask your healing team or guides to pass on this message for you. Do this by taking a few deep breaths to relax yourself. Ask your healing team to come forward and join you, then read the letter out loud and thank your guides. Trust that your message has been sent, and that your guides will pass on your words in some form or energy to the individual concerned.

- Allow time to pass. I'm sure you have heard the saying, 'Time heals all wounds.' This means that time offers us a chance to reflect on our experiences, prompting insight and the ability to move forward. Emotional healing takes time, just like physical healing – it's not an overnight process. Distance creates freedom, the freedom to be yourself.

- As important as it is to seek comfort from family and friends, an aspect of self-care that may be overlooked is having time to ourselves. This helps us to rebalance and protects our energy. It's okay to have limits and to have rest or downtime, because these limits help us defend our physical, mental and emotional health, and are needed so that we don't completely burn out or become overwhelmed.

- As adults we sometimes overlook the comforts of a soft toy or blanket. These childhood objects help you to reconnect with your inner child, and if you had a comfort object as a child you are never too grown up to pull it out again or to get a new one. These special items may help you feel happy and comforted, and to foster positive childhood memories.

Take up a healing art:

- Practise meditation. This helps in many ways, too many to list. What it does for you is unique to you. It can be used as a way of disciplining the mind and accessing your true self.
- Reiki is a form of Japanese energy healing which is a subset of alternative medicine. The Reiki practitioner uses a technique called palm healing or hands-on healing to transmit or conduct universal life energy to the person receiving the treatment, to encourage emotional, spiritual or physical healing.
- Take up yoga. Like meditation, yoga is a way of controlling and stilling the mind, and the various postures foster harmony in body and mind.
- Similar to yoga, Tai Chi combines deep breathing, relaxation and gentle flowing movements. It is often described as meditation in motion and has many of the same benefits.
- Try this simple exercise daily to promote gratitude. Every day, find two things in your life that you are thankful for. These could be material things you have, the presence of a loved one, the body that your soul inhabits, or an aspect of your body – anything that you like. You can repeat the things that you are thankful for – there are no rules. Now feel grateful for these things. By doing this, you place yourself in a flow of receiving, a flow of abundance and a flow of healing. By looking at what you have, you are replacing a sense of lack and anxiety with a sense of strength, and your energy begins to change.
- Remember, it's perfectly fine not to always feel spiritual, or to feel somewhat disconnected; it comes with living on earth and having a human experience. Just try your best to take care of yourself. Below I have created a recipe for love tea to support your self-care.

Easy love tea recipe for healing, love, harmony and peace
Enjoy this tea on any occasion; it supports self-love and aids in calming the body before sleep or meditation. If you and a loved one have had an argument or disagreement, this tea may help to bring balance to you both, offering some relief.

For one cup of tea you will need:

1 teaspoon rose petals
1 teaspoon camomile
1 teaspoon lavender

Begin by placing the herbs into a bowl and mixing them together.

Then take a few deep breaths and place both your hands in a cupped position over the bowl.

Set your intention – for example, 'I open myself up to divine love.' Then visualise white light going into the tea from your hands.

Now you can either put all the ingredients into a pan and boil on the hob for ten minutes, or use a tea pot, or add the ingredients to a disposable tea filter bag.

You can add honey for sweetness if you like.

Please note, it's important to research any herbs you are considering ingesting. If you are taking medications or have a physical condition, do ensure that the combination is safe for you to use.

A word about Solfeggio frequencies

The ancient Solfeggio frequencies have been shown to provide amazing healing benefits. When listened to, they have the power to influence the subconscious and conscious mind, bringing balance to the energy bodies and clearing blockages. These frequencies are believed to have powerful transformative effects. Pain and tension are softened while awareness and inner peace are enhanced, and the amount of love energy is increased. There are different Solfeggio tones, each one being associated with a different healing benefit. Some of the most popular ones are listed below:

- 852hz – returning to spiritual order
- 432hz – heightening perception
- 741hz – awakening intuition
- 639hz – connecting with others and strengthening relationships
- 417hz – accessing change
- 396hz – letting go of fear and guilt
- 174hz – releasing pain and healing the aura

The solfeggio frequency that I have personally found most beneficial is the 528hz miracle tone. This beautiful sound aids with rapid healing, transformation, and letting go of negative patterns. Below I have created a meditation that can be practised while listening to the 528hz miracle frequency. Its purpose is to support you with deep relaxation while observing without judgement how your body feels. It offers the opportunity for you to connect with yourself, the divine 'I am' presence. This tone can be found on YouTube (for free) along with all of the other frequencies listed above.

- Begin by finding a comfortable space to lie down, playing the 528hz in the background at a volume that suits you.

- Before you close your eyes, allow yourself to take a moment to feel the comfortable spot you are lying in. Feel the softness of the bed or sofa, relax and enjoy the sensation of comfort.
- If any thoughts come up, notice them and watch as they drift by.
- Let your whole-body merge with the surface beneath you.
- Try not to think about it too much. What you are doing here is allowing yourself to feel.
- Ask your healing team of guides and angels to come in and support you.
- When you are ready, begin by taking a few deep breaths in through your nose and out through your mouth.
- Repeat this until you find yourself becoming completely relaxed.
- Now, either in your mind or out loud, repeat the mantra, 'Divine healing light, fill me with your bliss.'
- Repeat several times – as many as you like.
- Observe how your energy begins to shift.
- Do not take too much notice of it. Instead, if you find your mind wandering, take your attention back to your breath, or continue to repeat the mantra, 'Divine healing light, fill me with your bliss.'
- Now imagine your whole body is being filled with loving, warm light.
- See this light being sent down from the deep cosmos, and streaming gently into your third eye chakra, like a waterfall of pure white light.
- When your entire body is filled with glowing light, allow yourself to bathe in its magnificent feeling.
- When you are ready, feel this light flowing out of the soles of your feet and spreading out into the universe.
- Take a few more deep breaths, and when you are ready, open your eyes.

- Take a moment to sense your surroundings.
- Thank your healing team for being with you.

Repeat this meditation as often as you like – you may find that you experience something different each time.

Final words

Although we experience pain at different levels, it is a common feature we all share, that is determined by our reaction to certain emotions, like resentment, anger or grief. While pain is something that we all have to experience, either emotional or physical, it is important for us to see that pain is placed along our path for us to experience it, and, once we get a taste or sample of what we don't like, we can then gravitate towards things we do like, although some people often do become trapped in or addicted to pain. Keep an open heart and allow illumined love to pour from your heart centre. When negative emotions arise they won't last, they can't because there is no space for them to linger when you shine from within. Eventually, the issue you face can just float out of your mind, and by then you know that you are in a different vibrational place.

The narcissist teaches you the wonders of love and how powerful it is to be in a place of unconditional love for yourself and for them. This truly brings harmony and peace. If you do not hold resentment in your heart, and instead have faith, love and let go, God shines light into your life. When you have reached a place of healing karmic entanglements, there is a greater strength within you. Releasing karma allows newly activated light to eliminate lower-level feelings, creating peace and confidence. Part of our own unique destiny involves karmic ties and past life energy, whether these be with people, our job, addictions or something else. Many of us have been repeating cycles in particular areas for many lifetimes, but once we end the karmic loops, we have the opportunity to dive into the realm of infinite possibilities where we can begin to create our own destiny.

Once you are able to transcend major karmic influence, you no longer need that vibration any more. This is one reason why you are here – to transcend your own karma so that you can then step into the true self. It is important that you know, 'Yes, I can do this.' Begin to see yourself in every human being, because really there is no separation between any of us. We are all connected, and the bonds we create with others always last within our heart space.

There is no past or future – there is only the eternal now. This eternal now reflects any healing instantaneously and becomes the living vibration. Magic and miracles can become the reality for us all by trusting that whatever is truly needed will show up when you are ready, with quantum downloads carrying energy of information designed specifically for what you need for your healing. Spirit and the universe communicates to you in ways they know you can understand, and you are able to receive hints along your journey. This could be through dreams, synchronicities such as seeing repeated numbers, or a simple inner feeling. Know that if you see any synchronicities this is a way of revealing you are in alignment and on the right path.

As previously mentioned, relationships are important, from the relationship we have with our family and friends to the relationship we have with our career. We talk a lot about letting go and trusting in the universe (God, source, or a higher power) that things work out for our highest and best good, and this is always the best way.

Repairing relationships and finding forgiveness is another important key in healing karma and bringing peace into our life. This doesn't necessarily mean that the relationship should go back to how it was. It means that you see the importance of having certain individuals in your life, and the purpose you served for each other. If you are unable to do this, continue to fill yourself with love via your heart space and mind, and send the same to them if you can. In doing this, you have the opportunity to break the karmic cycle, and to let go when the time is right for you. This is not necessarily to try and change anyone – rather, to have acceptance for the situation as it is. Never assume that a person will change under your influence. Change only happens if a person is willing, and wants to change themselves. Instead, allow the power of unconditional love to create your reality. Try to have no judgement, because it is judgement that keeps us from unity. Yes, all of us do judge; this is a feature of the ego mind. Instead, when any negative judgements come up change them to something positive. For example, if you see someone walking down the street and you don't like their hairstyle, acknowledge that thought then look for something you do like, perhaps something they are wearing. The law of attraction responds to love. As does everything that is living. Divine timing is always perfect, and when the time is right, repairing a relationship can be easy once the cycles have played out between you both, and there has been enough time to think about things and heal. This can be months, years or even in another lifetime, it all depends on you. When the time is right for you, any negative emotions such as guilt, resentment or shame will be released and you are able to make peace with yourself. This is the most important element of repairing a relationship, regardless of how it looks in the 3D; you have found peace.

When you have experienced the deepest grief it opens a door inside you so you appreciate happiness, and with each new cycle you go through, a powerful shift occurs within you, marking the beginning of even more opportunity to connect to the 'I am' presence. If you practise holding space for unconditional love, it will propel you into the desire to repair a relationship, especially those with whom you once shared a close bond. Remember, this doesn't necessarily involve you getting in contact with anyone – it simply means allowing your heart to be in a space of love. If you want to experience love, you must disconnect love with dependence on other people. Love has no connection with another person. It's all you. Instead, redirect your love towards life, and see how the world responds back to you.

Growth is a continuous process as we are infinite beings. I would suggest that you continue to find inspiration in different places to keep your vibration high and your spirit uplifted. Never limit yourself. Understand that beliefs can and will change as our awareness expands. It is time to leave outdated thinking behind – the power of true love is within you. Allow for unconditional love to extend to all your soul mates in your life, including the narcissist – even if that means loving them from a distance. Unconditional love means loving someone regardless of the condition or the outcome.

I wish you all the very best in your journey.
Paris xx

O-BOOKS

SPIRITUALITY

O is a symbol of the world, of oneness and unity; this eye represents knowledge and insight. We publish titles on general spirituality and living a spiritual life. We aim to inform and help you on your own journey in this life.
If you have enjoyed this book, why not tell other readers by posting a review on your preferred book site?

Recent bestsellers from O-Books are:

Heart of Tantric Sex
Diana Richardson
Revealing Eastern secrets of deep love and intimacy to Western couples.
Paperback: 978-1-90381-637-0 ebook: 978-1-84694-637-0

Crystal Prescriptions
The A-Z guide to over 1,200 symptoms and their healing crystals
Judy Hall
The first in the popular series of eight books, this handy little guide is packed as tight as a pill-bottle with crystal remedies for ailments.
Paperback: 978-1-90504-740-6 ebook: 978-1-84694-629-5

Take Me To Truth
Undoing the Ego
Nouk Sanchez, Tomas Vieira
The best-selling step-by-step book on shedding the Ego, using the teachings of *A Course In Miracles*.
Paperback: 978-1-84694-050-7 ebook: 978-1-84694-654-7

The 7 Myths about Love...Actually!
The Journey from your HEAD to the HEART of your SOUL
Mike George
Smashes all the myths about LOVE.
Paperback: 978-1-84694-288-4 ebook: 978-1-84694-682-0

The Holy Spirit's Interpretation of the New Testament
A Course in Understanding and Acceptance
Regina Dawn Akers
Following on from the strength of *A Course In Miracles*, NTI teaches us how to experience the love and oneness of God.
Paperback: 978-1-84694-085-9 ebook: 978-1-78099-083-5

The Message of A Course In Miracles
A translation of the Text in plain language
Elizabeth A. Cronkhite
A translation of *A Course In Miracles* into plain, everyday language for anyone seeking inner peace. The companion volume, *Practicing A Course In Miracles*, offers practical lessons and mentoring.
Paperback: 978-1-84694-319-5 ebook: 978-1-84694-642-4

Your Simple Path
Find Happiness in every step
Ian Tucker
A guide to helping us reconnect with what is really important in
our lives.
Paperback: 978-1-78279-349-6 ebook: 978-1-78279-348-9

365 Days of Wisdom
Daily Messages To Inspire You Through The Year
Dadi Janki
Daily messages which cool the mind, warm the heart and guide
you along your journey.
Paperback: 978-1-84694-863-3 ebook: 978-1-84694-864-0

Body of Wisdom
Women's Spiritual Power and How it Serves
Hilary Hart
Bringing together the dreams and experiences of women across
the world with today's most visionary spiritual teachers.
Paperback: 978-1-78099-696-7 ebook: 978-1-78099-695-0

Dying to Be Free
From Enforced Secrecy to Near Death to True Transformation
Hannah Robinson
After an unexpected accident and near-death experience, Hannah
Robinson found herself radically transforming her life, while a
remarkable new insight altered her relationship with her father, a
practising Catholic priest.
Paperback: 978-1-78535-254-6 ebook: 978-1-78535-255-3

The Ecology of the Soul
A Manual of Peace, Power and Personal Growth for Real People
in the Real World
Aidan Walker
Balance your own inner Ecology of the Soul to regain your
natural state of peace, power and wellbeing.
Paperback: 978-1-78279-850-7 ebook: 978-1-78279-849-1

Not I, Not other than I
The Life and Teachings of Russel Williams
Steve Taylor, Russel Williams
The miraculous life and inspiring teachings of one of the World's
greatest living Sages.
Paperback: 978-1-78279-729-6 ebook: 978-1-78279-728-9

On the Other Side of Love
A woman's unconventional journey towards wisdom
Muriel Maufroy
When life has lost all meaning, what do you do?
Paperback: 978-1-78535-281-2 ebook: 978-1-78535-282-9

Practicing A Course In Miracles
A translation of the Workbook in plain language, with
mentor's notes
Elizabeth A. Cronkhite
The practical second and third volumes of The Plain-Language
A Course In Miracles.
Paperback: 978-1-84694-403-1 ebook: 978-1-78099-072-9

Quantum Bliss

The Quantum Mechanics of Happiness, Abundance, and Health
George S. Mentz
Quantum Bliss is the breakthrough summary of success and
spirituality secrets that customers have been waiting for.
Paperback: 978-1-78535-203-4 ebook: 978-1-78535-204-1

The Upside Down Mountain

Mags MacKean
A must-read for anyone weary of chasing success and happiness
– one woman's inspirational journey swapping the uphill slog for
the downhill slope.
Paperback: 978-1-78535-171-6 ebook: 978-1-78535-172-3

Your Personal Tuning Fork

The Endocrine System
Deborah Bates
Discover your body's health secret, the endocrine system, and
'twang' your way to sustainable health!
Paperback: 978-1-84694-503-8 ebook: 978-1-78099-697-4

Readers of ebooks can buy or view any of these bestsellers by
clicking on the live link in the title. Most titles are published
in paperback and as an ebook. Paperbacks are available in
traditional bookshops. Both print and ebook formats are
available online.
Find more titles and sign up to our readers' newsletter at
http://www.johnhuntpublishing.com/mind-body-spirit
Follow us on Facebook at https://www.facebook.com/OBooks/
and Twitter at https://twitter.com/obooks